Execute the Office

Execute the Office

the

Essays with Presidents

Colin Rafferty

BAOBAB PRESS

ISBN: 978-1-936097-32-6 (print)
ISBN: 978-1-936097-33-3 (ebook)

Library of Congress Control Number: 2020941585

Baobab Press
121 California Avenue
Reno, NV 89509
www.baobabpress.com

Typeset and Design by Baobab Press

for Lauren, Emily, and Clementine, citizens

Where are our Men of abilities? Why do they not come forth to save their Country?

~ George Washington on March 27, 1779 , in a letter to George Mason decrying members of Congress focusing on state matters in the midst of the American Revolution.

No, I don't take responsibility at all.

~ Donald Trump on March 13, 2020, in response to a reporter's question about delays in testing for COVID-19.

Table of Contents

Execute the Office

Preamble

I am standing at the entrance to American History.

People murmur in passing, on their ways up and down the Mall's sidewalks. Near a tall white obelisk, someone flies a kite with skill and grace, making it dive and loop and dance through the air. Other people wait in line at a food truck selling Philly cheesesteaks. I can see the steam from the hot sandwiches rise into the cold January air, here, outside the entrance to American History.

A year from today, the National Park Service will make the final preparations for the Presidential Inauguration. The stage on the Capitol steps, the chairs for those with tickets and connections, and the cordons guiding those without will all stand ready for the next day's crowd. The souvenir vendors will have their merchandise ready to sell, the Secret Service will make final adjustments to their security plan, just as designers will put their own last touches on inaugural ballgowns and suits.

The crowd may extend down to American History, but it depends. Sometimes the weather keeps people away; sometimes even rain, snow, subzero temperatures couldn't keep people away. Sometimes they fill the Mall past the white obelisk, where today the kite flier deftly makes the long tail spin into a fluttering spiral.

Today is January 19. A year and a day from now, someone will stand at the center of that stage, place a hand on a book, and take the oath of office: *I do solemnly swear that I will faithfully execute the Office of President of the United States, and will to the best of my Ability, preserve, protect and defend the Constitution of the United States.* At that moment, they make history. They enter American history.

That's in the future, though. Right now, I am the person about to enter American History, one of the nineteen museums of the Smithsonian Institution. In this building, we keep those items at the core of our identity as Americans: the Star-Spangled Banner and the Greensboro Woolworth's lunch counter, Edison's light bulb and Dorothy's ruby slippers, even a piece of Route 66.

On the top floor of the building, front and center, as if to underscore their centrality to the American narrative, we will find the exhibit on the American Presidency. In the nearly quarter millennium of America's existence, forty-four men have stepped into that role, some by design, some reluctantly, some by accident and happenstance. All of them were leaders of a country, symbols of America and its changing identity, and all of them were men, with desires and talents and flaws.

In the exhibit, visitors can see the artifacts that connect these men to the crucial moments in America's experiment with democracy. Near the entrance, we find the inkstand of George Washington, who, before he was the first president of the United States, was the president of the Constitutional Convention, leading the group that determined how this country would function. Beyond that, we see the top hat worn by Abraham Lincoln that night at Ford's Theater, when he was murdered by a man who hated that, with a stroke of a pen on a January day, Lincoln had proclaimed the emancipation of the men, women, and children enslaved in the rebellious South, thereby changing and challenging our ideas of who is an American. In a display case to the side, we can see the file cabinet from a psychologist's office, its drawers wrenched open by a team of burglars, setting into motion a chain of events that would culminate in the resignation of Richard Nixon, the first president to leave the office that way.

More and more—photos of their families and their lives in the White House; their working relationships with (and sometimes against) the other two branches of government; their campaigns and their decisions, successes and failures, all collected at the focal point, front and center, of the National Museum of American History.

Perhaps we give them too much prominence, and yet, on the sidewalk, a year and a day before the next inauguration, a kite dancing in the air behind me, I am struck by these forty-four men as a way to understand this country. It's a representative democracy, after all—we are them. They stand for us. For good, or for bad, the president is the one we look to with the hope that he will lead the country forward.

I could go somewhere else. I could see machines that soar in the air or dinosaurs that roamed the Earth. I could see art from around the world, or I could see panda bears and Komodo dragons, or I could ride a carousel in front of a castle. I could leave the past and the presidents for another day, if I so chose.

Instead, I walk across the plaza, fifty state flags flapping in the wind. I pull open the door, and I disappear into American History.

The Virginia Reel

George Washington
First President of the United States
1789-1797
2 years since the Constitution
66 years until Emancipation
177 years until the resignation

The monument doesn't dance. The coin and the bill don't dance. The paintings and statues and silhouettes don't dance. The engravings, frozen; the profiles, motionless. The beds in which he slept, the tomb in which he lies, they don't move. The military uniform in the Smithsonian Institution's glass case stands still. Even the teeth, the legendary false teeth, are silent on their stand at Mount Vernon. Nothing is in motion.

But George Washington loved to dance. Not the George Washington we have imagined; not the nation's enshrined first president, first in war, first in peace, first in the hearts of his countrymen; not our idealized and adapted-to-any-purpose Founding Father; but the real, corporeal George Washington, the 6-feet, 2-inches, 175-pound George Washington—he loved to dance. He danced for hours with his generals' wives at balls held during the Revolution, and he danced with Martha even more—Martha, barely five feet. They must have made a sight on the ballroom floors of Virginia, of Philadelphia, of New York City, him gallant and her dainty, the contrasts in perfect harmony with each other as the musicians played their minuets and reels.

To dance the minuet, the reel, you have to know the steps. In America, we are always rediscovering the steps of the dance, trying to recreate it from the remnants we can find in our soil. It's difficult to discover the abstract, the human, from the bits and pieces that survive the years.

4

Here we are on the Northern Neck peninsula in Virginia, in front of a house, but looking at a shape outlined in white stones. Here, George Washington was born. You might arrive, as we have, and gaze at the Potomac River, the herons flying past, beating their wings to put themselves in motion. And you might look, as we did, at the house that stands on the site and think you are looking at George Washington's birthplace, because, after all, you have come here to the George Washington Birthplace National Monument, a National Park Service ranger has welcomed you, given you a map, told you that admission is free, so here you are, a house in front of you. This must be the place, here is where George Washington's step-grandson landed his boat and placed a stone that read, "Here, George Washington was born."

But it is not the house. It's the stones in front of the house. It's the white stones surrounding the outline of the missing house; *Building X*, they call it. X is the thing we are trying to solve for, the unknown parts of our heritage, the things we can't ever know but still try endlessly to figure out. X is the beginning of our questioning: *Who were they?* In front of the outline, you might, as we did, stand and try to determine the shape of what once stood there, the origin point of the father of the country. Every dance has prescribed steps, an order, but the first step of the Virginia reel is to admit uncertainty. We begin from X; it marks the spot from which we take the first step.

I should have known this when we visited. We were living in Fredericksburg, Virginia, across the Rappahannock River from the farm where Washington had grown up. There was no cherry tree there, no evidence for the story of *I cannot tell a lie*. There was no coin buried in the soil on the other side of the river, no evidence for the story of his mighty throw. At the farm, they had only found the site of the house in 2008, the year before we drove out to the birthplace. They had found the house's foundation and its trash pile, the midden. They only had fragments of what had been, only the outline of what had stood on the site.

In the midden, they found broken pieces of crockery with a cherry tree motif.

We learned this at a talk by the site's chief archeologist at the local public library that summer, a talk also attended by a man dressed as George Washington, a man who arrived and announced, "I'm here to see what you've found out about me," who sat patiently through the whole lecture, whose cell phone rang during the Q&A. He looked at it, turned it off, and said, "It's Thomas Jefferson. He'll call back."

We are always recreating George Washington. We make him whatever we want him to be—America's first conservative, America's original liberal. Slave-owning plantation master. Securer of our liberties. Military genius. Agricultural mogul. In the city named for him, only Washington's monument doesn't look like him, only four blank white surfaces upon which we can project whatever we like, onto which we can exhibit what we've found out about him.

Even in the reel, he is a creation: shaped by his brothers' deaths, which make him a prominent landowner; shaped by his youthful work as a surveyor, which makes his body powerful, teaches him the land, teaches him to understand how a man, or thousands of men, might move across it; shaped by his wish to transform himself by copying his own set of rules of civility from a sixteenth-century French Jesuit etiquette manual (Rule #19: *Let your Countenance be pleasant but in Serious Matters Somewhat grave.* Rule #67: *Detract not from others neither be excessive in commanding.* Rule #89: *Speak not Evil of the absent for it is unjust.*) Even the false teeth (or at least the only remaining complete set) were a patchwork of lead, ivory, and teeth from animals and other humans.

This is Washington: out of many, one. A man, a real person, to bring the idea of the United States of America, with all its contradictions, into existence. When he takes the oath of office in New York City, the first time anyone speaks the words that make a citizen president, he has only one of his own teeth in his mouth. He speaks those words with not only his tongue and his lips and his tooth but also the teeth of animals, the teeth of men and women and children, the teeth of free men and possibly the teeth of slaves. He speaks the words of the oath with all of us, out of many, one, *e pluribus unum*, the motto of the United States.

You need many people to dance a minuet, to dance the Virginia reel, to move elegantly across the ballroom floor. You need musicians and servants and cooks. The dances could go all night and into the next morning. You served food for the hungry, drinks for the thirsty. You provided for everyone. You showed them how it could be done.

Washington had absolute power for life in his hands on two occasions, and both times he relinquished it voluntarily. He resigned his military commission at the end of the Revolution, even though some of his officers wanted to make him king. He stepped down from the presidency after two terms, even though he could easily have won a third term, even though he could have stayed in the office until he died.

In reading stories of the presidents, I have seen how power, great power and small power, changes people, how it can transform a young man from a poor Kentucky farming family into President Lincoln, and how it can change a man, born into the wealthy Roosevelts of New York, into a fighter for illumination in the rural South. I have seen the famous, the infamous, and the obscure lust after power, throw their lots in with the bigoted, as Millard Fillmore did, and the greedy, as Warren Harding did. I have seen powerful men undone by drink, like Franklin Pierce; by their desires, like Bill Clinton; and by their own paranoia, like Richard Nixon. I have seen how power corrupts the bad and challenges the good, and how that is a fundamental part of human nature. That makes George Washington, who gave it up twice, even more remarkable to me.

But he owned human beings. He participated in slavery for his entire life. His beloved Marquis de Lafayette begged him to free his slaves, and he did not. When the capital was in Philadelphia, he brought his slaves with him and was careful to send them back to Virginia before they had stayed long enough to be emancipated under Pennsylvania law. He questioned slavery, evolved his views on it, privately supported gradual emancipation. He freed his slaves in his will, but only the ones he owned, and only upon Martha's death.

Martha owned many more than he did, and they were not freed upon her death.

This is the step I stumble on, the part of the dance I cannot follow, the thing I have found out about him. He is so good. He owns human beings. He is human, he is flawed. In any context, this is an extraordinary flaw.

Washington is our alpha, our zero milestone. All the presidents who have followed him, all those who will, are measured against him. Almost all have fallen short, but they have helped us understand him better. They have helped us appreciate him more. They have illuminated his flaws, and because the United States is a representative democracy, they may help us understand ourselves more, just as we hope that we might cause them to understand themselves. In the many, the one.

Why do we dance? We dance for pleasure, for joy, for celebration. We dance for social reasons, for commemorations of transformation. We dance for the possibility of connection with another human being.

So let's dance with Washington and those who follow him. Let's do our best to follow the dance's steps and see him not as a statue or a portrait or a white obelisk, but rather as a human being. Let's do our best to converse with him and them, following Rule #88: *Be not tedious in Discourse, make not many Digressions, nor repeat often the Same manner of Discourse.* Let's pay attention to our partners, follow their leads, see where it takes us. At some point in the evening, we'll switch to a new partner, and the dance will continue, as it has, as it might still, well into the early hours of the morning.

Our dance closes by returning to the starting position. We keep starting over with Washington, keep trying to find all the pieces. We walk around the perimeter of the ghost house where he was born. We dig through the middens to see what we can find out about him, we will call him back with our findings. We pay our admission fee and walk the grounds, tour the house, climb his stairs, see the bed in which he died. We visit all the cities and towns named for him, the schools, the mountains, an entire state. George Washington slept here. George Washington sleeps here. Here is a man with 110 rules, the last of which exhorted *Labour to keep alive in your Breast that Little Spark of Celestial fire Called Conscience.* Here is a man who died with 317 enslaved people working on his property.

Dance complete, we bow to our partners. We walk off the ballroom floor, out the door, across the bowling green, into the museum. We approach the teeth in their case like pilgrims. We look at the teeth, lead, ivory, animal and human, and we listen for what—for whom—we will hear next.

Reiteration

John Adams
Second President of the United States
1797-1801
10 years since the Constitution
62 years until Emancipation
173 years until the resignation

John Adams served as the second president of the United States from 1797 to 1801[1].

---

1   Facts are stubborn things; his life is no different. No matter what else he did in his long career—lawyer, delegate to the first and second Continental Congresses, signer of the Declaration of Independence and the Constitution, author of Massachusetts' own Constitution, ambassador to the Netherlands and France during the Revolution and Great Britain afterwards (imagine the gall as the first former colonist, short, undignified, approaches King George III), the first vice president—when it comes to the ways we rank the great men of America, the ways we try to tell our story through our leaders, John Adams will always be the second president. Pope Linus followed Peter, Bert Hinkler followed Charles Lindbergh, Buzz Aldrin followed Neil Armstrong, and Adams replaced the irreplaceable Washington. Try to follow those footsteps. Try to take the office when the most beloved American of the country's short history has relinquished power. This is the crux of things: we restart every four or eight years with someone new. It doesn't always work. Of the nearly four dozen presidents, how many could we call great? How many are just footnotes? When you are the second, you will always be compared to those who came before you. You will always find yourself compared to the trailblazer, the pioneer, and very often, you will be found lacking in comparison.

    Adams can never be Washington, so the temptation to reinvent is real. When he takes office, he has already disentangled himself from one George; to do so with another, retired to Mount Vernon, will not trouble him. Adams loves pomp and circumstance, relishing power in a way Washington did not. He will become his own man; he builds the navy and avoids war with France. He fights with Jefferson and his own party; he is the first president to live in the Executive Mansion in the newly created District of Columbia. He raises a son who will also become president. He will die on the Fourth of July, fifty years to the day that he broke with the past by putting his name to parchment. For decades, he will be counted among the footnotes, trapped between two towering titans of the presidency, but then a single book will make a convincing argument for reassessing him and restoring his good name, the one on that parchment from 1776. And although that name itself has faded—the ink almost vanished, barely legible in the low light of the National Archives—John Adams remains, an interruption, a continuation, a reinvention, a reiteration, even to this day.

The Apologist

Thomas Jefferson
Third President of the United States
1801-1809
14 years since the Constitution
54 years until Emancipation
165 years until the resignation

The miracles are all missing. The mammoths are extinct. Forgive me, Thomas Jefferson, for how I use you now. Forgive me my trespasses, how easily I see others ascribe words to your mouth that never left it, how they claim that you said *eternal vigilance is the price of liberty* or *bad government results from too much government* or *the Bible is the source of liberty* or *speech that condemns a free press are the words of a tyrant*. See them bend you to their own arguments for small government, for big government, and forgive me the way that I say nothing in your defense. Forgive me the way I hold your contradictions, your "all men are created equal" rubbing against the slaves of Monticello, your "pursuit of happiness" against your "dusky Sally." Forgive me the time I spent in the muse-um looking at your homemade Bible, all the miracles cut out, all the moral teachings left. Forgive me the ten years I spent in a school run by a church. Forgive me my church, my state. Forgive me that I do not head into the wilderness, keeping watch for the wooly mammoth, the way you instructed Lewis and Clark to do. Forgive me when cashiers do not recognize the two-dollar bill as legal tender. Forgive me, for what this country needs is a good five-cent cigar, a moment of peace bought with a portrait of you. Forgive me, for I have seen your Dec-laration under bulletproof glass, and I don't know how a living docu-ment can breathe when it is trapped in noble gas, a kind of elemental aristocracy. Forgive me, for I have forgotten the joys of France. For-give me for laughing at Freedom Fries. Forgive me, Thomas Jefferson, for the times I have become you: when I spend too much, when I take too much pleasure in food and wine, when I make my own Louisiana Purchases and do not ask permission.

Forgive me, Thomas Jefferson, Sage of Monticello, for you had such plans for this country, and I do not know that we have fulfilled them. On the campus of what they still call "Mr. Jefferson's University," we have painted words of accusation on your statue in the middle of the night, *RACIST + RAPIST*, and the defense for libel is to show the veracity of the statement. Near your university, there is a memorial for a young woman who died when a white supremacist struck her with his vehicle.

Thomas Jefferson, did you curse this country when you opened up a Native burial ground on your property so that you could explore how they buried their dead? When you declared a *wall of separation between church and state*, what else did you build? Thomas Jefferson, why do I look to you to forgive us when perhaps you should be the one asking for forgiveness? Kennedy said that a gathering of Nobel laureates was the greatest gathering of talent in the White House except when you dined alone, but I look at the results of this grand experiment of democracy, and I'm sorry to say that I observe only turbidity.

Paul Jennings Dreams of the Burning of Washington

James Madison
Fourth President of the United States
1809-1817
22 years since the Constitution
46 years until Emancipation
157 years until the resignation

A house set on fire has its own smell. There is the wood, of course, but also the paint on the walls, the heavy fabric of the curtains, the rugs. There is the furniture, stuffed with horsehair and upholstered with silk, which will burn both fast and slow. The provisions in the kitchen, meat and flour and spices, which will carry their own tributaries of scent into the river of smoke billowing from the Executive Mansion.

It will all burn. Even before the British add more fuel, even before the winds fan the flames, it will all burn, except for the few items rescued by those who stayed behind. Whatever they can load into a cart, whatever they can carry, only that is what will be saved. The burden of choice. Those who stay behind will save a few things—red silk curtains and the silver service, the blue and gold Lowestoft china reserved for state dinners, and a few other things—but everything else will be consumed, from whatever art and desks and chairs remain down to the food and wine young Paul Jennings had laid out on the table for the guests of James Madison, architect of the Constitution, president of the United States, and owner of young Mister Jennings.

Fifty years from that August night in 1814, fire again burns through the country. Lincoln will have freed the slaves held in rebelling territories. Grant will have Petersburg under siege, feeding men into the conflagration. And Paul Jennings will be sixty-five, a free man, finally emancipated by a new owner decades after trying and failing to purchase

14

his freedom from the widowed Dolley Madison. When he dies at seventy-five, he will have lived his life as Lincoln said the Union could not: partly in slavery and partly in freedom.

That lies ahead. At the beginning of the evening, there is only the threat of fire: tinder, kindling, sparks, flints, and steel. Madison evacuates early, telling Dolley to be ready at a moment's notice. The moment is not long in coming. The British, led by Sir George Cockburn, approach from the north, torches alight. They will burn as much as they can. The Capitol. The president's house. The Library of Congress. They do not burn the newspaper, but Cockburn will level its building, smash the presses, and destroy all the Cs in the type cases, so the journalists cannot write about him.

Dolley moves quickly. When the moment comes, she instructs the servants—both slave and free—to gather what they can. She shoves some of the silver into a large bag. Take what you can. What you can lift. What can be loaded.

Young Mister Jennings helps two men—Mister Sioussat, the doorkeeper, and Mister McGraw, the gardener—take down Gilbert Stuart's larger-than-life portrait of George Washington, breaking the frame to move more quickly. They load it onto a cart, add whatever else will fit, and then depart. Even if he is fifteen years dead, and even while the city with his name falls, they cannot allow Washington himself to fall into enemy hands.

The city burns through the night, but a violent thunderstorm extinguishes the flames the next day. Cockburn pauses, wondering at divine intervention. By this time, the Madisons and the servants and the slaves are safely away.

White men make their wars, and what falls to the women, and the workers, and the slaves is to preserve what needs preserving.

Paul Jennings works as Madison's valet until Madison dies. He lives with Dolley in the rebuilt Washington, where he encounters the large free Black community, which he will join upon buying his freedom in 1846. He plans a slave revolt, which fails, and works for the

Pension Bureau after the Civil War, in which his three sons fought for the Union. He publishes the first White House memoir, his own, and buys a house, a kind of American dream. His family continues. Almost two hundred years after that August night of fire, the descendants of Paul Jennings gather at the White House to see the painting he helped load onto a cart and drive away from the destruction.

Scent is the sense closest to memory. Who is to say that on some nights in his house, the elderly, free Mister Jennings did not smell the wood burning contentedly in his fireplace and suddenly return to that night, with Mister Sioussat and Mister McGraw and Mrs. Madison, with Cockburn on the advance, with his muscles aching from the speed and strain of the night, with his hands remembering the feeling of the rolled-up canvas, the coolness of the silver, and the roughness of the cart? In front of the fire, he may dream of the past, his past and ours, his dream of a life saved from the fire, of silver and a painting and what all of us can carry when the hour demands it of us; perhaps he dreams of how, on the cart, he looked back while moving away from the raging fire, the destruction, and how, unlike Lot's wife, he lived.

He lived. The city was not swept from the plain. Perhaps he remembered, instead, how once he had been the property of one man, and then the property of that man's wife, and then the property of yet another man. Perhaps he remembers how he had been born in shackles and how he had cast them off, and how in looking back upon ruination, rather than become the pillar of salt, he became himself, Mister Jennings, finally, at last, pillar of the community, pillar of the family, a man whose descendants would return to the house where he once worked, his blood returning one more time, this time free, this time carrying only themselves and what they chose to bring with them.

The Eye of James Monroe

James Monroe
Fifth President of the United States
1817-1825
30 years since the Constitution
38 years until Emancipation
149 years until the Resignation

In *On Photography*, Susan Sontag writes that "photographs are a way of imprisoning reality . . . one can't possess reality, one can possess images—one can't possess the present but one can possess the past."

The idea of photography—using the sun to capture an image on a light-sensitive material—predates the United States, but only in the 1820s does a Frenchman named Nicéphore Niépce think to fix the image to the surface in order to preserve it for posterity. Even then, his process requires hours, even days, to succeed, far too long for any human to sit for a portrait.

In 1839, Niépce's associate Louis Daguerre announced that he had refined the process into the daguerreotype, the first public instance of the photograph. A picture would only take a few minutes to develop; the first two humans photographed are captured in a street scene, one standing still while the other shines his boots. Now we have a record of what people actually looked like. No longer is the burden of representation placed on a painter's interpretation of the sitter.

None of this matters for James Monroe, fifth president of the United States, who died on the Fourth of July eight years earlier, in 1831. Like the first four presidents, and unlike every president after him, the image of James Monroe is not captured in a photograph, only in paintings and engravings. When all we have is a painting, an interpretation, what—if anything—is the true image? Asked another way: how real must an image be before we accept it as authentic?

John Vanderlyn's portrait of Monroe hangs in the Gallery of Presidents in the National Portrait Gallery in Washington. The painting isn't far from the famous Gilbert Stuart portrait of George Washington, and only a little bit farther away is, at the time of writing, the newest arrival, Kehinde Wiley's portrait of Barack Obama. People line up to take their picture with Wiley's Obama, and stand far enough back to fit all of Stuart's Washington into the screen of their phone. Vanderlyn's Monroe watches from the side, his blue eyes gazing into the distance. His forehead is slightly furrowed, his chin prominently cleft. His visible sideburn seems to sweep back into his ear just a little, the hair shot through with silver strands.

Not too far from the National Portrait Gallery, Samuel Morse's portrait of Monroe hangs in the White House's collection. Painted a few years after Vanderlyn's Monroe, also during Monroe's presidency, Morse's Monroe looks off to his left with eyes somewhere between blue and gray. His hair is uniformly dark, unrulier, and something about the shape of his head is different from Vanderlyn's Monroe. They don't look like the same person, except for the chin.

In 1954, a government employee engraves a picture of James Monroe for a five-cent stamp. This Monroe doesn't look like either Morse's or Vanderlyn's Monroes, except for the cleft chin. His hair seems to be entirely white and swept up, like a preview of Andrew Jackson's famous portrait. His eyes are blue, but that might just be because the entire stamp is printed with blue ink.

Three James Monroes. Already, you can see that we are on tricky ground. We can say that we know James Monroe because we know the facts of his life. But a painting is only a collection of pigments carefully arranged on a surface. It's an interpretation. It's not James Monroe. It's a painting of James Monroe. And if a biography is similar—a collection of facts arranged on a page, can we ever fully know James Monroe, and by extension, anyone?

Monroe was born in 1758 in Westmoreland County, Virginia, on the estate next to the Washingtons. Today, no building remains.

Eighteen years after his birth, in 1776, Monroe joins his former neighbor in crossing the Delaware to attack Hessian troops. He's the young man holding the flag in Emanuel Leutze's *Washington Crossing the Delaware*, the famous painting of that scene. It hangs in the Metropolitan Museum of Art, occupying almost an entire wall. He's wounded in the attack, one of only a few presidents wounded in combat.

Monroe encounters war again, thirty-six years on, as James Madison's Secretary of State. He follows Madison as president; most secretaries of state did then. He was the last president to wear breeches instead of pants. None of the paintings show his breeches.

His biggest accomplishment as president is the Monroe Doctrine—which you've probably heard of—which warns Europe to stay out of the Western Hemisphere's affairs.

He writes it with his Secretary of State, John Quincy Adams, who—as you've probably guessed—follows him in office.

He dies in New York City on the Fourth of July, 1831. In 1858, his body was moved to Richmond via steamship and a hearse drawn by six white horses, and then buried in an ornate tomb. As far as I can tell, there are no photographs of this; even almost two decades after Daguerre's announcement, a steamship and trotting horses would have been moving too fast for the light to capture them on the plate.

Consider instead, the first photo of a president, a photo of John Quincy Adams, Monroe's successor. The photo allows us to know, in a way that a painting does not, what Adams looked like with reasonable accuracy. We can confirm the white hair surrounding a bald head, the white sideburns. We can see the downturned corners of his mouth and his piercing gaze. We can see the gnarled fingers woven together, the black pants, even a glimpse of his socks. We can look at these things and know them for certain. We might feel that we possess John Quincy Adams and his socks more than we possess James Monroe.

We know so little about the presidents. The oldest recording is of Benjamin Harrison, which means we don't know what half of them sounded like. Lincoln's voice was reputedly high-pitched. We have no idea what Jefferson sounded like, or Madison, or Grant.

Not until almost the twentieth century do we know what a president looks like in motion. Another forty-five years, and they come into our homes via television. The first president to be photographed by a digital camera was Obama, which, like Carter being the first president born in a hospital, feels ridiculous to consider.

Even the presidents we know in living color, sound, and motion—what do we really know about them? We know they are human, and therefore they seem familiar to us, perhaps even more so than our friends and families. Sometimes I feel like I know more about what the president is doing than I do about most of my extended family. But even the walking, talking, photographed person is still a creation put together by the images and sounds we take in. How real is this amalgamation?

We have our ideas of the president, and then there is the president himself: human, and therefore complex beyond knowable.

I'm not looking at the eye of James Monroe. I'm looking at a painting of the eye of James Monroe. You're reading a description of two paintings and an engraving of the eye of James Monroe.

In Leutze's famous *Washington Crossing the Delaware*, the light is wrong. The ice is wrong. The river is too wide. The people standing—including the future presidents—would have fallen into the river. Historically, Monroe wasn't even in the same boat as Washington.

Any portrait—Vanderlyn's or Morse's or mine—is always incomplete and unfinished. There's no way to fit everything into the frame. Completion is a task as impossible as the stance Monroe has in a boat in which he never set foot.

We cannot know what it was like to be him, or to be any of them. What did his eye see? The ice of the Delaware pushed aside as the boat glided silently toward Trenton? The page on which he wrote his doctrine slowly filling up with ink? His wife, Elizabeth, as First Lady another public figure, in their quiet moments alone?

These moments are not ours to witness. We can imagine. We can try to understand. But we cannot see. It was never fixed upon the photographic plate.

They are the mystery, the humanity, and since we have nothing to possess, no reality to imprison in the photograph, we must leave it to them.

Self-Portrait with Slave Ship

John Quincy Adams
Sixth President of the United States
1825-1829
38 years since the Constitution
34 years until Emancipation
145 years until the resignation

On the day he sits for the first photograph of a president, John Quincy Adams is not the president and has not been the president for fourteen years.

On the day he sits for the first photograph of a president, John Quincy Adams weeps over his late mother, visits a female seminary, shakes about one hundred hands, gives a speech, meets a dwarf dressed like Napoleon, and gets a small rock lodged under his eyelid. This is one day as described in his diary, which is less than what actually happened but more than what's visible in the photograph. He was president. In the photograph, he is a congressman.

That's present tense: August 1, 1843. John Quincy Adams is past tense. We think of him, if we think of him, in the past. We have no regular reminders of him, the way we do with other presidents, but he spans the opening chapters of America. George Washington appoints him minister to the Netherlands; he meets Abraham Lincoln when they both serve in Congress.

There's history in this family, chronicling, observing. Family trait. His father, the second president, and his mother, the second First Lady, wrote to each other during the Revolution. His grandson, Henry Adams, will describe the dawning of the twentieth century in his autobiography. On this August day, nearing the midpoint of the nineteenth century, here is John Quincy Adams, sitting for a photograph.

Past tense again. He went everywhere. Traveled to Europe with his father during the Revolution. Minister to the Netherlands, Prussia, England, and Russia, when going to these places by boat and carriage took months of journeying.

Future tense: 138 years after the day John Quincy Adams's photo is taken, I will be five years old, visiting Washington. I will remember little of this trip—a cab, a hotel restaurant—but I will clearly remember a moment of a film in the Smithsonian's Air and Space Museum, a locomotive approaching the screen. I will not remember the moon rock or the Apollo 11 capsule. I will not remember the *Spirit of Saint Louis* hanging next to the Bell X-1. I will not remember the Wright Brothers' flying machine. Apart from that snippet of film, I will not remember a single thing in this museum, which opened the year I was born and which contains very little that existed during John Quincy Adams's lifetime, and yet was built because, in part, of John Quincy Adams.

The Smithsonian exists because James Smithson, an English chemist who never visited the United States, makes a bequest to the United States to create an institution of learning. The Smithsonian also exists because John Quincy Adams ensures that the funds are used to follow Smithson's wishes.

Past tense: as president, Adams was thwarted by his enemies, but as congressman, he found his turn to be the thorn in the side. He fought slavery. When the Congress instituted a gag rule preventing the introduction of anti-slavery petitions, he introduced pro-slavery petitions in order to speak against them. When his fellow congressmen threatened to censure him and remove him from his chair of the Foreign Relations Committee, he called their bluff, telling them "I have constituents to go to who will have something to say if this House expels me. Nor will it be long before gentlemen see me here again!" In other words, any attempt to make his presence in the House a thing of the past would ensure his future presence in the House. They did not censure him.

Future tense: the man in the photograph of 1843 will be perhaps visible in a mural that will be painted in 1938 by Hale Woodruff at Talladega College, an institution of learning founded by former slaves. Woodruff will paint three murals depicting the *Amistad* mutiny, in which captured Africans rose up and slew their captors. No one in the middle panel of the mural—the trial scene—resembles the photograph.

We are comparing a 1938 painting of an 1841 event to an 1843 photograph. Some layers of representation are in play here. We carry in our minds the idea of anything when we first learn of it: the *Amistad* trial, a museum building on the National Mall, John Quincy Adams himself. Then we see a representation of it, perhaps a painting or an etching or any of the ways images traveled before the photograph, and our idea shifts. Then, if it exists—as it does not for Washington or Jefferson, Madison, Monroe, or even Quincy Adams's own father— we see a photograph, an interpretation, to be sure, but one that we recognize as a generally trustworthy, generally accurate representation of the idea, and our idea shifts once again, like water trickling through the limestone bedrock of a building, finding its way inside.

Past tense: on February 24, 1841, John Quincy Adams spoke for four hours in front of the Supreme Court in defense of the *Amistad* rebels. After his closing argument, he remarked on the passage of time and how he had last argued in 1809 "before the same Court, but not the same judges—nor aided by the same associates—nor resisted by the same opponents," all of whom he had outlived. He prayed that the current justices might go to their "final account with as little of earthly frailty to answer for as those illustrious dead."

The rebels were found not guilty and repatriated to Africa.

Present tense: let's finish with the photograph taken on August 1, 1843, in New York. We may look all we like, understanding completely that this is indeed John Quincy Adams, who had, fourteen years earlier, been the sixth president of the United States; we may read his diary and know what happens just before and just after this (and how odd that both involve his eyes, the weeping and the injury); we may lay our own futures over him, his photographs, his representation and invisibility in a mural; we may consider him the bridge between the Father of the Country and the Great Emancipator; we may see him, the first president to ride a train, at the start of another bridge that leads to a small boy watching a train on a film in an institute dedicated to the exploration of the sky and beyond. But finally, we will see in this picture only an old man, the time before him and the time after him both history and mystery, both clear and opaque, a past, a past, a past, a present, a future, a past.

Death Song for Andrew Jackson

Andrew Jackson
Seventh President of the United States
1829-1837
42 years since the Constitution
26 years until Emancipation
137 years until the resignation

Because he died at home, in bed. I have seen the bed.

Because "Trail of Tears" is the closest this country has to a shorthand for genocide, for national shame.

Because he set in motion the removal of native tribes in 1830. He played the role of "Great White Father," but an abusive father, one who strikes a child and says *It's for your own good* and *This hurts me more than it hurts you* and *You'll thank me one day.*

Because he helped make this country great in so many senses of the word. Because, like Walt Whitman, poet of America, he contained multitudes. Because, like Whitman, the words he spoke shaped America.

Because he dismantled the National Bank.

Because he fought the States' Rights advocates.

Because he defied South Carolina's claim to nullification.

Because he paid off the entire national debt.

Because he said "Our federal Union—it can and must be preserved," and it shocked the room to hear a son of Tennessee say that.

Because he did these things, and made this country great, and because the reasons for this country's greatness include the stolen labor of Africans and the stolen land of its natives, I sing this death song for Andrew Jackson, not a song of life, like Whitman (*I sing myself, and celebrate myself / and what I assume you shall assume / for every atom belonging to me as good belongs to you*), but a song of death.

Because I sing him and I do not celebrate him. I do not assume we share all beliefs. I do not know to whom the atoms belong.

Because we spent a week in grade school on the first Thanksgiving.

Because I learned about the Sand Creek Massacre from a placemat in a Colorado restaurant and not a history teacher.

Because I live in a state where people argue that a football team is a tribute and never seem to understand that tributes are for the nearly dead or already vanished.

Because when we spend twenty dollars, we see a man who held the country together and who destroyed nations.

Because I cannot dismiss him outright, because his adopted son, Andrew Jackson Junior, was a native boy, I sing this death song.

Because I believe that an essay can sing, that it can take the ordinary clay of fact and breathe life into it.

Because I believe that Andrew Jackson is all the parts of America, a boy during the Revolution, a war-wager, a campaigner, a grieving widower, a stone-cold killer with both a gun and a pen, he is Whitman with a tiny waist, he is small, he controls multitudes.

Because I am a white man writing about another white man, neither of us even the one-sixteenth that some claim, both of us failing the blood quantum.

Because I believe in the telling of the story, in finding the right arrangement of the facts, in the history of our federal Union—it can and must be told.

Because somewhere in our seventh president is the key to America, in how he wept for his wife and condemned thousands, in how he defended the Union and defied the Supreme Court. Whitman said that *He most honors my style who learns under it to destroy the teacher.* Jackson created the next version of America, the one that followed the Revolution. He transformed us from rebellious child to stern father.

Because he died at home, in bed, after enforcing Indian Removal for 46,000 natives. I have seen the bed. It is small, comfortable. He was a small man. He had a good death. He did not starve, he did not freeze, his body did not end up buried somewhere on the plains. He died in a bed. I have seen the bed.

I sing this song in passing here. For Andrew Jackson, and for me, and perhaps you. Perhaps this pull between the good and the bad, preservation and destruction, the legacy of a land given to us by fathers who took it, perhaps these are our shared atoms.

I sing my song of barbarism across the rooftops of the world. I send these words out to find a home and to rest in the unease of Jackson. A yawp, a death song, an essay, a poem, and now I think I understand what Whitman meant when he left unanswered the question *Have you felt so proud to get at the meaning of poems?*

My song is done.

State of Alarm

Martin Van Buren
Eighth President of the United States
1837-1841
50 years since the Constitution
22 years until Emancipation
133 years until the resignation

There is a story about Christmas 1835 in the Jackson White House. Vice President Van Buren plays games of tag with the Jackson children, and at one point, he must stand on one leg and chant *Here I stand all ragged and dirty, / if you don't come kiss me I'll run like a turkey!* No one does, and so the man who will be president-elect by next Christmas runs after the children like the bird. He "strutted like a game gobbler."

Consider him at that moment, when he realizes that no one is coming to help. He plays a game, and the rules say that he must attempt to chase the children. Consider him as he lowers his leg and takes the first awkward, tentative step forward.

Here's where we lose the script, wander off alone into the American wilderness. Martin Van Buren, president thanks to Andrew Jackson's endorsement, walks the halls of the Executive Mansion on Inauguration Day, 1837, all alone. Jackson back to Tennessee. Quincy Adams in Congress, an enemy from the other party anyway. His wife, dead almost twenty years, and his children, three of five who make it to adulthood—all gone.

He is alone, too, in a way no president has been before, because Madison dies at his home just nine months before the Inauguration, and with him gone the primary knowledge of the Founding Fathers is gone. Whatever Washington knew—or Adams or Jefferson or Franklin, or Jay or Hamilton—it's all lost when Madison dies. Now here is Martin Van Buren, son of Kinderhook, New York, alone in the

Executive Mansion, the first president born in an independent United States of America. He never knew the struggles to birth the country.

Is this where the slide toward disunion, toward the guns of Fort Sumter and Shiloh and Gettysburg begins? For the first time, a president cannot ask the Constitution's authors *What did you mean? How does this work?* Within a generation, we will be at war with ourselves. When does the rickety fear inside our hearts, the dread that all of this may one day fall apart, when will it take hold?

Almost certainly not on that day in March of 1837. Van Buren is continuing Jacksonian politics, keeping the Union preserved by working with the South and its original sin, what they call their *peculiar institution*, which must not be disturbed.

Still, his footsteps echo in the hallway. Alone too often.

When we search, and do not find, when does the fear arrive? The initial shock, the redoubled efforts, the sorrow of solitude, the false bravado, the breaking-down. Behind them all, that concern, that worry. A year and a few months from that Christmas, and Martin Van Buren walks the Executive Mansion halls. What is his mood? What is the nation's?

All these things compound. The price of cotton falls. The land bubble bursts. Speculation out west collapses. Reliable sources of currency become unreliable. Could Martin Van Buren have predicted this? They used to call him the Little Magician for the way he could manipulate politics. They used to call him the Sly Fox for his cleverness. They used to call him Old Kinderhook—O.K. (this is how this term came to prominence) for his birthplace. His wife, Hannah—she called his name with a soft Dutch accent: *Maarten*.

Now they call what's happening all around him the Panic of 1837. Now they call him Martin Van Ruin. Now they sing *Van, Van, is a used-up man*. Now sounds the alarm. Now comes the moment when he might look to the past for answers and find only the tombs of the Founding Fathers. Now comes the moment when he might look into the future and see only a dark cloud gathering to the south. He will stand at the helm of the state and try to steer it forward, through the storm.

He gets four years. He tries for eight, but the Whigs nominate a popular general. He tries again in '44, but the dark horse Polk surges past him. He tries again in '48, a Free Soil Party man. But nothing. And when he dies, the country is split. Robert E. Lee will have forced George McClellan to withdraw from the outskirts of Richmond. In Old Kinderhook, Martin Van Buren's heart will finally be overtaxed, his breathing spent. Whatever awaits him on the other side, whatever awaits our country, he will not know. Perhaps he does not dread it either. Here he stands, all ragged and dirty, no more guesses to make, no more steps to take, no more games to play.

Time, Cut Short

William Henry Harrison
Ninth President of the United States
1841
54 years since the Constitution
22 years until Emancipation
133 years until the resignation

Let's keep this brief:

William Henry Harrison, Indian killer, Jefferson's agent, territorial governor, Whig hero, ninth president, falls sick, dies thirty-two days after inauguration. Call him Tippecanoe, call him Tecumseh's killer. He burned the Shawnee to the ground, discredited the Prophet. He did this of his own accord, as he must in this time. There is no such thing as a drone, no such thing as a mother of all bombs. It is all axes and flintlocks. To kill a man, you have to see him. When you see a man die, he dies in front of you, you see him, his eyes glaze, his chest settles into itself. There is no death from a remove; a smoothbore musket is accurate to about a hundred yards. There is only the real blood of the man in front of you on your real hands, and Harrison's hands are wet. Ohio is frontier. Indiana is wilderness. Years later, he campaigns, the first candidate, promoted with a hard cider bottle shaped like a log cabin; he is of common roots, you see (a campaign lie—Harrison is actually plantation-born, twelve dollars and fifty cents to tour today). President through violence, his death sets precedent; Tyler follows, assumes the mantle, promises to execute the office and protect the United States of America, though he'll vote to dissolve the Union two decades hence.

At the end: in one hundred and five minutes, he breathes out his promises, breathes in the rain. Three weeks later, he takes ill. Nine days later, he dies. A drowning on dry land. Opium/leeches/castor oil/snakeweed. Pneumonia/jaundice/septicemia. Tecumseh's killer

31

has poison for blood. Tippecanoe has liquid for air. Dead in the middle of the night, dead in the White House, lamplight on the walls painting the scene. This is an era when you die at home, when the physical reality of death is so much closer than now. Harrison dies at home, surrounded by doctors and family. Again, no distance from death.

American Falls

John Tyler
Tenth President of the United States
1841-1845
54 years since the Constitution
18 years until Emancipation
129 years until the resignation

The view is better from the other side, but he refuses to cross over the river border, so great is his hatred for the British. He's content to see the falls from this limited view, to watch the Horseshoe thunder from a distance. The other set, American Falls, is better seen from the Canadian side; but on the American side, where John Tyler stands, he can see from whence the water falls but not where it lands. It's a problem of perspective. A problem of vision. A problem of not knowing where the story ends, only how it begins.

The ground is falling away. Horseshoe Falls grinds down the clay of the riverbed by almost four feet each year.

Tyler's here only because he steps forward when the ground disappears. Harrison dies, and Tyler says: *I am president. I am not acting president, or temporary president. I am the president.*

And it works. The ground stops vanishing. The Congress does not take control of the executive branch, as some thought they might. He is president.

But nature is a force. The erosion starts again. This is an era when Congress, not the president, is the most powerful branch of government, and its speaker, the man called Clay, wants control. Tyler won't fall into step with his party, won't go over the falls in a barrel so the Whigs can run the country. Clay tells him he cannot use the veto as Jackson did, and yet Tyler vetoes the reestablishment of the National Bank, leading to almost his entire cabinet resigning two days later. He vetoes increased tariffs, twice, and the Whigs leave him behind to stand with Clay. Tyler's abandoned, a man without a party, adrift. The visit to Niagara is a ritual performed by presidents, an incantation against collapse, against the forces of history, which are the forces of nature. *Keep us whole*, they say. *Keep us together.* At the place where America ends, the Chief Executive prays for unity.

Tyler loses the flow. His party leaves him, nominates another man for 1844, although Tyler still runs for the office.

Finally, it crashes, splinters on the rocks below. Tyler retires. Older, he chairs the Virginia Peace Convention in 1861. Without regrets, he votes for secession, to dissolve the Union. He had taken the oath of office when Harrison died, had sworn to defend the Constitution of his Union. And yet, and yet, and yet all that falls away. He dies in Richmond two years later, a citizen of what believes itself to be a foreign country, buried in a foreign land, far from Horseshoe Falls, far from the vanishing ground, buried, at last, in the solid earth.

State of the Union

James K. Polk
Eleventh President of the United States
1845-1849
58 years since the Constitution
14 years until the Emancipation
125 years until the resignation

"In performing for the first time the duty imposed on me by the Constitution of giving to you information of the state of the Union and recommending to your consideration such measures as in my judgment are necessary and expedient, I am happy that I can congratulate you on the continued prosperity of our country."

—first State of the Union address, 1845

The State of the Union is red. The State of the Union is warlike, blood-tinged. The State of this Union is unknown to you in the present day, the long smear of history obscuring your view between the Revolutionary War and the Civil War. The State of the Union is red with exertion, expansion, with Texas annexation, with the incursion of foreign troops upon American soil (the red-faced shame of invasion, even invented; the red-faced fury of invasion, even invented). The State of the Union is, as regards Mexico, *not of the American character which it is our desire to cultivate with all foreign nations*. The State of the Union is a man from Tennessee, James Knox Polk, asking Congress for a declaration, receiving it, sending men into war's red mouth. The State of the Union is Ulysses S. Grant and Robert E. Lee serving in the same army, future blue and future gray covered by the red of war. The State of the Union is the Halls of Montezuma; the State of the Union is an occupied Mexico City; the State of the Union is one thousand, seven hundred and thirty-three men killed in battle in less than two years, a generation of soldiers practicing the tactics they will eventually use against each other. The State of the Union is red, and read, meaning a written document delivered to Congress from the president, as established by Jefferson (Jefferson, always better read than heard), as it will be until Wilson addresses Congress in seventy years. The State of the Union is words arranged in an order to create an effect, a tactical plan, a charm offensive, straight talk to the American People via their representatives, for Polk, always something red.

"As the wisdom, strength, and beneficence of our free institutions are unfolded, every day adds fresh motives to contentment and fresh incentives to patriotism."

—second State of the Union address, 1846

The State of the Union is white. The State of the Union is a sullied white, a stained white, a white working overtime to maintain its existence. The State of the Union is a white president who owns human beings and seeks to preserve that peculiar institution. The State of the Union is a white man who owns more than fifty men at his death, fewer than one hundred days after leaving office. The State of the Union is a question we have asked for its entire existence: how are we to live together as equals? The State of the Union is a line drawn between the numerator and the denominator, three-fifths, a line Mason and Dixon trace onto the map, a line extending into the territories—beneath this, above that. The State of the Union is an eight-percent cash profit on his plantation; the State of the Union is more than half of his slaves' children dying before age fifteen. The State of the Union is a meeting between past and future as fellow congressmen John Quincy Adams and Abraham Lincoln oppose Polk's war and its expansion of slavery, an attempt to keep the peculiar institution that pulls this country apart from growing into new territories. The State of the Union is white, a surrender, a giving-up. The State of the Union asks, what can we do? The State of the Union says this peculiar institution simply is—nothing to be done.

"It has ever been our cherished policy to cultivate peace and good will with all nations, and this policy has been steadily pursued by me."
—third State of the Union address, 1847

The State of the Union is blue. The State of the Union is below. The State of the Union promises one term only, serves one term only. The State of the Union is true blue, is loyal. The State of the Union is hiding its weaknesses, its fractures. The State of the Union does not have long—twelve years until that congressman from Illinois is inaugurated and the guns fire on Fort Sumter, fracturing the Union. The State of the Union will become the blue of the sky above the fields of Shiloh, Antietam, Gettysburg, filling with cannon smoke as the battles progress. The State of the Union is a bluish tinge on the lips of the dying Polk, dead three months after leaving office, a man who never sees what his work and words have wrought.

"It may, indeed, be truly said that my Administration has fallen upon eventful times."
—fourth State of the Union address, 1848

The State of the Union is an acronym, SOTU, a continuance: *so, too.* The State of the Union goes on. The State of the Union endures. Listen to what the president says each year as Congress and cameras watch: *The State of the Union is strong,* the president will likely say. The vice president will clap from behind. Depending on the election, the Speaker of the House may or may not applaud. The State of the Union is strong. The State of the Union endures. The State of the Union asks how are we to live together? And well, what now? Well, what now?

Antaeus

Zachary Taylor
Twelfth President of the United States
1849-1850
62 years since the Constitution
13 years until the Emancipation
124 years until the resignation

Not the divine right of kings, but the endless potential of democracy, the idea that the leaders may grow from any home, that, native-born, they are of the soil of America. Seven presidents have been born in log cabins; five in hospitals. The log cabin is our mythopoetics, the place from which our idea of The American comes.

Zachary Taylor's mother births him in a log cabin that served as an outbuilding for the Montebello plantation in Virginia. He was born in a humble place next to a magnificent place, an apt metaphor for the presidency. Anyone over the age of thirty-five who is a natural-born citizen of the United States can become president. Since 1787, only one non-white man has done so. Those numbers will change, I think. After his birth in a log cabin, Zachary Taylor went to Kentucky, joined the army, became a general, led troops to victory in Mexico, parlayed that into a political career (as Washington and Jackson and William Henry Harrison had before him), was elected president, and died two years into his term, likely from cholera contracted by eating cherries and milk on a hot Fourth of July in Washington. He is buried in Kentucky in a military cemetery.

Antaeus, the giant of Greek mythology, held his outsized strength only as long as he remained in contact with the earth, an apt metaphor for a president. For centuries, we needed them to remember their roots, where they came from, the earth from which they were pulled. We needed them to attend the state fair and witness what wonders the

38

earth has brought forth. We needed them to wear blue jeans, eat the same food that we do, have the common touch. Be in touch. Touch us. Do not be out of touch. And thereby stay in power.

Is this still true?

On the day a baby was born to Barack Obama, Sr. and Stanley Ann Dunham in Kapiolani Medical Center, August 4, 1961, thirteen presidents—or men who would become president—were alive. Kennedy was in office, Johnson his vice president. Eisenhower, Truman, and Hoover all rested in retirement. Nixon contemplated running for governor of California, where a movie star named Ronald Reagan made speeches against Medicare for the AMA. Ford was a former football player-turned-congressman from Grand Rapids, Carter a peanut farmer in Plains, George Bush an oil company president in Houston who had just sent his son George W. to boarding school in Massachusetts. Donald Trump's parents had just sent their fourteen-year-old to New York Military Academy to try to manage his behavior. In Hot Springs, Arkansas, a high school student realized he'd never play the saxophone as well as he wanted, and so switched to public speaking. Later, he took his stepfather's last name of Clinton.

I am not telling you this to make you consider the past. I am telling you this because probably the next seven or eight presidents are already alive. Not born in log cabins like Taylor and Lincoln, or plantation homes like Madison or Harrison, or family houses like Wilson and Eisenhower, but in hospitals, like Carter, Clinton, Bush Jr, Obama, Trump, and likely you. There is so much of America in this idea of the birthplace—ideas of class and technology and health care, of who survives and who does not, of who we count as a "real" American and who we do not. Antaeus forced travelers through his land to wrestle against him, which seems to me an apt metaphor for how we consider the experiment of America, how we can—and perhaps should, perhaps must—wrestle with this country while we are in it.

Zachary Taylor owned slaves and was the last president elected from the South until LBJ, a gap of 116 years. He could not have conceived of a black man becoming president. He could not have conceived of a woman running for president. The country changes.

Hercules defeated Antaeus by lifting him off the ground and crushing him in a bearhug. This seems to me an apt metaphor for the presidency's effect on its holders, how they are crushed by the weight of the job. This job murders men.

Zachary Taylor was followed by rumors of poisoning. He was exhumed one hundred forty-one years after his death, and the autopsy showed no evidence of this. He was returned to his mausoleum in a military cemetery in Kentucky with full honors.

Zachary Taylor was born in a log cabin next to a plantation. He became a general, then president. He ate cherries and milk on the Fourth of July near the half-built Washington Monument, and they made him sick, and he died from that sickness. On the day he died, fourteen presidents, past and future, were alive. This seems to me an apt metaphor, but perhaps we no longer need a metaphor to understand that, for us, the peoples in the land and of the land, in all centuries and in all seasons, time passes in ways both quick and slow.

500 Black Ships

Millard Fillmore
Thirteenth President of the United States
1850-1853
63 years since the Constitution
10 years until the Emancipation
121 years until the resignation

You don't know him, or know him only as a shell, a funny name, a repeated pair of consonants. You know he was president, but just sometime, you're not sure when. You don't know anything he did.

I'll explain.

He's the first president born in the nineteenth century, the first born after George Washington dies; there's a significance to this, a continuity, the idea that the country is more than its founders. He's the second vice president to become the president after a death. He's the last Whig president. He signs the Compromise of 1850, which adds California to the Union as a free state and organizes the land taken in the Mexican-American War into the Utah and New Mexico territories, delegating to them the decision on slavery ("The Union Is Saved!" cry the people upon the news, eleven years before the war begins).

It's his name on the letter from the United States that Commodore Perry carries when the black ships sail into Tokyo Bay on the last day of March 1854. Perry turns away all the emissaries the Emperor sends to the ship; he'll meet only with the Emperor himself, occupant of the Chrysanthemum Throne, the man descended from Emperor Jimmu, the first Emperor of Japan, descended himself from the sun goddess and the storm god.

This is what I hope you will remember: wealthy men and their corporations sought to open Japan to the West, and as the president was a means to those ends, these men considered Millard Fillmore the equal to a living god.

His signature's lovely, calligraphic elegance, the swash added to the top arm of the F swirling out over the M, doubling back to meet the dot of the I. The first name, waves cresting, black ink a ship's path on the paper. He had the biggest library of any president up to that point. He signed his name in each book, marked its shelf number in each one. Methodical. Complete.

In the same year that Perry opens Japan with Fillmore's signature, the painter Kano Kazunobu begins a series of scrolls, one hundred total, of the five hundred disciples of the Buddha, commissioned by a temple in Edo. The disciples—*arhats* or *rakan*—are capable of amazing feats. A dry river flows again. The lotus flower grows from a begging bowl. Stones rain from the sky to end conflict. The *rakan* fly on foxes.

They travel between the six realms: gods and demigods, humans and animals, hell and the realm of the hungry ghosts, consuming, consuming. When an earthquake kills seven thousand people in Edo in 1855, the *rakan* use tiny dragons to blow out the fires, while people escape from their collapsed worlds.

The hungry ghosts are the reincarnations of those who have died having done evil deeds of a certain kind—not those bad enough to warrant rebirth in hell or as an animal, but bad enough to keep them from a peaceful state. Desire, greed, ignorance—these are the sins of the hungry ghosts.

Kazunobu works on these paintings until his death nine years later. He almost finishes the series; after his death, his wife and his own disciple work from his sketches for the last ten. Methodical. Complete.

Everything happens slowly, with the deliberation of Kazonobu making his hundred paintings. Fillmore's an accident, president only because of a hot July 4 and some cherries and some milk. By the time the black ships reach Edo and Perry demands that Fillmore's signature be presented only to the Lotus Flower Throne (although the Shogunate, and not the emperor, is the true leader of Japan at this time), he is no one again, retired to the city by the crashing water, the city of the Falls. Franklin Pierce, a drunkard consumed with sorrow, takes his place.

The nation Fillmore once led slides toward war, world collapsing, and he is headed toward obscurity and embarrassment. In his final notable act, he runs for the high office again on a campaign against the foreign, calling himself a Know-Nothing, presenting himself as against the foreigners, the invaders, who arrive not in five hundred black ships but in the ports of the East Coast. At his career's end, Fillmore is driven, like the hungry ghosts, by something that prevents him from a peaceful rest. Maybe power. Maybe greed. Maybe the knowledge of his former godliness.

And Kazunobu's paintings too. They are installed in the temple, survive the firebombing of Tokyo in the second World War, although the temple is badly damaged. In 2011, the public sees the hundred scrolls for the first time, and in 2012 they travel, in a reversal of Perry's ships, back to Washington. The Smithsonian Institution sells out of the exhibition catalogue.

Once, Fillmore was a god's equal; then, nothing. What sorrow that must be. Every man who is president is president, whether by election or by accident. Nothing can remove them from the paintings, the forty-five disciples of the Constitution. They perform the amazing, but only briefly, and then they are men again.

When Perry arrives, Japan is unknown, the mysterious East. And now we know more of Japan than we do of Millard Fillmore, the hungry ghost, once capable of magic, now capable of nothing. Write your name in the book. File him away on his shelf. Use your method. His story's complete. A tiny dragon will blow out the flame.

Diagnosis

Franklin Pierce
Fourteenth President of the United States
1853-1857
66 years since the Constitution
7 years until Emancipation
117 years until the resignation

Patient: Thirty-seven-year-old white male, married, father of two (a third died in infancy), who has recently resigned his Senate seat (Democratic, New Hampshire) due to frustration at becoming a member of the legislative minority. Patient has been in Congress ten years, first as representative, then senator, in a career that embraced the Constitution and states' rights. Patient fought the National Bank and infrastructure improvement, allowed abolitionists to deliver their petitions but not read them. Patient supported the gag rule; now he finds himself gagged. Patient expresses a desire to focus on his law practice and his family, especially in the wake of his infant daughter's death.

Diagnosis: Thwarted ambition.

Treatment: None. This is America, 1842. We have had the railways for only fifteen years, which means that we only now understand what it feels like to move faster than a galloping horse. We are the first generation in human history to know this. We cannot bridle ourselves at this auspicious moment. We must expand to the west, toward the setting sun, so that it may never set on us.

Patient: Forty-two-year-old white male, married, father of one (a son has died from typhus), who has recently returned from the conquest of Mexico, where he served as a brigadier general. In battle, his horse stumbled and fell upon his leg, injuring it. Soldiers believed the patient

44

to have fainted from fright. Patient convinced his commanding officer to allow him to ride into the next battle; however, despite tying himself to his saddle, patient lost consciousness again due to pain. Upon his return to New Hampshire, patient received a hero's welcome in Concord but still reports feelings of inadequacy and sorrow.

Diagnosis: Paranoia. Depression. A sadness not dissimilar from the feelings of inadequacy that plague us all.

Treatment: More brass. More marching. More bunting. More banners reading "General Franklin Pierce: Our Hero." More sights and sounds to remind a man, to remind everyone, of the country's glory and goodness, and to drown out the ever-louder litany of failures.

Patient: Fifty-two-year-old white male, married, now childless, fourteenth president of the United States, who recently suffered trauma in a train wreck after his election. Unbeknownst to his wife, Patient allowed his name to be placed into nomination for the Democratic election; his wife fainted upon hearing the news that he had received the party's nod. After the election, the train carrying the soon-to-be First Family derailed near Andover, rolling down an embankment. Patient's only living son was crushed, head almost severed, the body visible to the patient and his wife for quite some time. Patient is a combat veteran, but both he and his wife report great distress over the sight of their son's mangled body, as well as a subsequent sense of separation between them; patient's wife stays to her own rooms in the Executive Mansion, dresses in black, does not speak with the public.

Diagnosis: Soldier's heart. Battle fatigue. Melancholy. Someday, post-traumatic stress disorder. Someday, depression. Recognition of the fact of life's fragility, of what can be torn apart in the ordinary moment.

Treatment: Diversions to occupy the mind, to push away the image of the son's near-severed head (it never goes away). Anything to occupy the hand and mind: a hobby, a pastime, a bottle if he must (he will). Despite his traumas, he must fulfill his job's requirements, to preserve the Union from being torn apart and to reconcile its differences, its half-slave and half-free nature. Patient is from the North and supports the South's right to own human beings. These are desperate times. Patient is a desperate man. The man and the hour have met.

Patient: Sixty-five-year-old white male, widowed, childless, former president of the United States. Patient complains of a pain inside him, a scarring that will not allow him to live much longer. During his presidency, the patient caused Kansas to bleed by signing the Kansas-Nebraska Act into law, allowing for popular sovereignty to determine whether that state would allow slavery, inciting a hemorrhaging of political, then actual, violence that spilled into the entire country. This resulted in Patient's party abandoning him at the convention, nominating instead a man who had spent years abroad as an ambassador, untainted by the blood of Kansas. Patient warned that abolition would tear the country in half, that the North must back down, and instead he has seen his nation rent, then made whole, an impossible physical feat that nevertheless has occurred at the hands of Abraham Lincoln, against whom the Patient had spoken. In these days, Patient has turned to both bottle and religion as a means to make sense of what he has seen and what he has lost.

Diagnosis: Cirrhosis. Sorrow. A great emptiness inside him. An inability to understand how time has passed him by, as it will all but the greatest among us.

Treatment: Nothing to be done. The country is its setbacks as much as its successes; sometimes even more so. All that remains to be done is to make ready for what lies ahead, to leave him to the past, abandon him and his ideas for the new frontier. Our beauty lies in the way we might choose to go forward, the way that we might look at our difficulties and forge ahead into the battle. Our beauty emerges in the moments when we make the hard choice, follow the road not taken, explore the wilderness. Our beauty lies in our willingness to go on.

Joist

James Buchanan
Fifteenth President of the United States
1857-1861
70 years since the Constitution
2 years until Emancipation
113 years until the resignation

What holds a house together: a solid foundation, a careful framing, attention to details, a willingness to repair, a sense of how it all fits into the landscape. *A house is a machine for living in*, said the architect Le Corbusier a century after James Buchanan's presidency.

At Mount Vernon, they will tell you the story of Washington's greatness; at Monticello, of Jefferson's ingenuity; at Montpelier, of Madison's practicality; at the Hermitage, of Jackson's derring-do and love for his wife. At Wheatfield, James Buchanan's home in Lancaster, Pennsylvania, they will tell you of his compromises and accommodations, of how one half of the house looks like a southern plantation and the other half looks like a northern manse, and how he would greet his guests at whichever door he thought they might find more welcoming.

His job, as he saw it, as the men who elected him saw it, was to hold the house together, a task at which he failed and against which we still judge him. A northern president who sought to appease the South and its slaveholders, to find a way to keep the walls and ceiling and floors from collapsing into rubble and splinters while still preserving its cracked foundation—the one comprised of three-fifths and the Fugitive Slave Act and the Wilmot Proviso and Dred Scott and westward expansion and a million other additions and precedents, the weight of which proved too much and brought the walls tumbling down. *A house divided against itself cannot stand*, his successor said in a speech. A house divided against itself is a machine in the process of breaking down, overcome by friction and wear and mechanical failure. A house divided against itself is where he lives.

If we can draw a metaphor between the house and the country, then we can also dare to draw a metaphor between the house and Buchanan himself, how he might have felt divided against himself and the world, a public face versus a private face, how he lacked the words to describe who he was, a bachelor in Washington, the subject of whispers and rumors. When we discuss him now in positive terms, it is in this half-visible, half-hidden notion of who he might have been, a gay man, or a bisexual man, in a time that forced a kind of invisibility on him and the senator from Alabama connected to him, their relationship an open secret in the corridors of power.

He served one term. The Union dissolved as he passed the reins to Lincoln. Three years later, he could hear the cannon fire from Gettysburg, less than sixty miles distant. Perhaps, as the battle to resolve the questions he could not, would not, address, rages a short distance from him, he would walk to the frog pond at the edge of his property and watch for a while as they splashed and croaked, performing their froggy feats. Perhaps he came to their pond regularly, watching them through the seasons, from egg to tadpole to frog, metamorphosing or dying as nature required of them. They change, and in changing, they survive. What Buchanan did was attempt to avoid change, to avoid the collapse, and instead, the collapse arrived, as machines must always break down. Thermodynamics in action. He tried to save a house by keeping it as it had always been, but that is no machine for living in; it is a museum piece, a shrine to the past, an unnecessary saving. It cannot, it could not, it did not stand. What lets a house fall? A cracked foundation, a shaky framework, ignoring what's obvious, rot in the wood. Neglect, inattention, malice, and good intentions.

Three Sentences on Failure

Abraham Lincoln
Sixteenth President of the United States
1861-1865
74 years since the Constitution
Signed the Emancipation Proclamation in 1863
109 years until the resignation

Near the end of his two-hour speech at the dedication of the cemetery at Gettysburg, the dirt still churned and turned open from the battle four months earlier, Edward Everett quotes Pericles: "The whole earth is the sepulchre of illustrious men." And maybe at this moment, Abraham Lincoln, who has been patiently listening or allowing his mind to wander this whole time, a two-page speech in his pocket, himself just a year and a half from the sepulchre, maybe at this moment he notices Everett at the podium, framed against the Pennsylvania sky, and thinks of what he is about to do, about to stand and say to this assembled crowd, about how the reporters will report on his speech, about how the word might go out into the world from the page, over the wires, just as his orders from the War Department do, and about how right now, for just a few more moments, he is the only person who knows what he will say here.

"The whole earth is the sepulchre of illustrious men," but this earth holds the ordinary men who died either close to or far from their homes, on Union soil at least, unlike the men from Indiana and Iowa and Lincoln's own Illinois who have been buried in Virginia and Tennessee and other states in rebellion; Lincoln knows this is their war, ultimately, that they are the men he sends to fight and die, his three hundred thousand more who die because he asks them to do so, and this is his tragedy forthcoming, Booth's single-shot derringer holding the single shot that will make him one of the war's last casualties, giving him over to the angels, putting another illustrious man into the earth.

And Everett finishes, and the crowd cheers, and Lincoln arises to speak (a photographer captures this, the closest we have to a photo of Lincoln speaking at Gettysburg), putting his hat on his head and reaching into his pocket for the speech, ready to unfold it and deliver, ready to admit what he cannot do, what he and all of us will to do, which is to commemorate and consecrate and hallow—and just before the moment he speaks the first six words, a mathematical question to be memorized by junior high school students for decades to come, maybe at this moment he thinks of Pericles, first citizen of Athens, leader in another war; maybe he thinks of the whole earth, of the "sepulchre of illustrious men," of his hometown of Springfield and his own place in the earth—maybe he thinks of all these things, looks at the Pennsylvania sky once more, and speaks.

Warp and Weft

Andrew Johnson
Seventeenth President of the United States
1865-1869
78 years since the Constitution
2 years since Emancipation
105 years until the resignation

At a point—some night, most likely the day's cutting and sewing and stitching done, tomorrow's work ahead of him—the idea becomes clear, snaps into focus in front of the young tailor's eyes. A moment, when in the light of a candle, his wife over his shoulder guiding him, he looks at the scratchings in front of him, lines like jagged stitches:

XXXXX XXXX XX XXXX XXXXXXXX

He is a tailor, he is good at putting things together, and he recognizes—he *reads*—a word in all of that mess. Perhaps a simple word like *the*, *he*, or *she*, or perhaps his name. Perhaps he points to the word, sounds out its phonemes, looks up to his wife, who smiles at him, saying, *Yes, Andy, that is your name, Andy.*

In that moment, Andrew Johnson, illiterate tailor of rural Tennessee, looks at the page beneath him, and confirms that yes, he is emerging from the page:

XXXXX XXXX XX ANDY XXXXXXXX

He is a tailor, a good one. Years from now, when others could do it for him, he mends his own clothing. He looks at a bolt of cloth and sees it unfurl into shirts, dresses, a coat here and a pair of pants there. He sees patterns, where to cut or to stitch, where to bind, or where to rip a seam apart. He sees how to use as much of the cloth as possible, how to reattach a sleeve so the stitches do not show. He has not needed to read for this, but when his wife teaches him, he understands both that the marks on the paper mean something, and that whatever they mean, they mean a station beyond a tailor's.

He reads. The world opens to him. What had been XXXXX, he now recognizes *Eliza*, his wife, his teacher. He had known his state's name, but now he sees written *Tennessee*, the pattern of repeated letters, the way a pen moves when writing it. He reads everything, books, newspapers, the Constitution, whose XX XXX XXXXXX becomes *WO LKU RUQRIU* and finally resolves into *We the People*, and where he encounters another word, potentially for the first time, emerging from the shadows: *impeachment.*

Because of the customers who come into his shop, he has learned to speak well, and he begins his ascent—alderman, mayor, the state house and senate, United States Congress. He buys a slave, his Constitutional right. He believes in the Constitution, believes in how these words, when read, form a more perfect union, the threads that stitch together the pieces of the union.

When it unravels, he holds fast the whole cloth. He can look at the jumble and make sense of it. Before the war, he had been governor; his successor cut the threads binding it to the Union, to Andy's beloved Constitution. When Grant and Pope and Buell tear much of Tennessee bloodily from the rebels, Lincoln names him military governor of his state, and then names him vice president for the '64 election, thinking already about Reconstruction.

But if we pull this ascending thread of his career, it takes all the stitches with it. He is likely drunk when he takes the oath as vice president, and a month later he becomes president when his own assassin loses his nerve while Booth leaps from the box. The task of binding up a nation's wounds falls to him, a tailor.

And yet the Constitution's friend would leave this to the states. The North sees him giving away the victory; the South sees him as hands-off, and they cut the patterns of Jim Crow from the cloth he gives them. He inherits almost an entire presidential term, and in his four years he clashes with the Radical Republicans in Congress, who see him as too gentle with the former rebels, who pass legislation over his vetoes.

Perhaps he is. Perhaps he knows that to pull too hard on a piece of fabric risks tearing it beyond repair. In the first two years of his presidency, the South, despite the abolition of slavery, begins to return to its prewar state, with former leaders and former laws and the new black codes designed to hold the freedmen back—slavery in a new change of clothes.

When the Radical Republicans solidify control of Congress at the midterms, they look to break the South. They place the states of the former Confederacy under military rule and pass rules to tie Johnson's hands together as president to prevent him from firing Cabinet officials who do not agree with him. When he fires Lincoln's Secretary of War, Edwin Stanton, the Congress impeaches him—the first time this provision of the Constitution ever comes into play—and he is acquitted in the Senate by a single vote. The rest of his presidency is unremarkable, scrap cloth on the pile.

What if a different self-taught southerner was president for Reconstruction? What if, instead of Johnson's would-be assassin losing his nerve, Booth decides not to go to Ford's Theater that April night, and Lincoln—kind, merciful Father Abraham—is the one to bring the country back together?

The answer is impossible to know, and all speculations are hazy guesses, like trying to look through muslin to see a picture clearly. It would have been different. It would not have been what Andrew Johnson did.

Andrew Johnson is buried in his Tennessee—stitched into an American flag, his head resting on a copy of the Constitution, his legacy a reminder that this country's lie—*anyone can be president*—means that the wrong person can become president, and that these ideas—all men are created equal, by the people, of the people, for the people, and that they shall not have died in vain—do vanish from the earth, and we forget how to read them. They fade from *ALL MEN ARE CREATED EQUAL* to *ALM MON ATE CLEVTEV EMUAL* to *TLR VXA ATR MNEBCZ JLPQT* and finally to simple lines at which we stare, uncomprehending.

Crossing the Rapidan

Ulysses S. Grant
Eighteenth President of the United States
1869-1877
82 years since the Constitution
6 years since the Emancipation
97 years until the resignation

I'm falling. I thought the ground was there, that
the wall would hold. I was wrong, and now I am
moving through the air, nothing holding me.

                         Grant moves south.
                         Grant moves south.

The sun is high in the sky, rising over my forehead.
As I accelerate down, I think, quietly: *I am*
falling.

                         Grant moves south.
                         Many thousands dead.
                         Grant moves south.

I had been mowing the lawn, moving backwards,
pulling the mower to get over a difficult-
to-reach area. And the stone wall—

                                    —hmm?—

—the wall that divides our yard from
the neighbor's—

Many thousands—

I backed over it. I fell, am
falling.

A shell lands, exploding
near Grant's HQ in the
Wilderness, his first stop
moving south. His aides
scatter. He doesn't move.

Time does slow. I can think
I am falling several times, can
think *how did this happen* before
the inevitable impact.

The many thousands: 2,246 Union dead,
12,037 wounded, 3,383 captured/missing. In two days.
All the earlier invasions of Northern Virginia
retreated back across the Rapidan after
incurring losses like these.

Me falling: picture the legs and arms
rising up, the back sinking down, leading
the way to the inevitable
at 6.8 meters per second, per second.

It's not unlike a body thrown across a field
by a shell explosion. It's not exactly it, *per se*,
but it's like it.

There will be a point of impact, of invasion—
where my back, just below the shoulders, will
meet the ground first, thousands of pounds of
force on my bones.

Grant tried where others failed, crossed the Rapidan.
He'd hoped to make it through the overgrown Wilderness
without meeting Lee but didn't. He lost 17 percent of his army
in two days. When the firefight set the forest alight,
the wounded burned.

Force = mass x acceleration.
Like a bullet.
Like a falling body.

The other generals had retreated. Hooker fell
back. Burnside fell back. McClellan (when
he fought) fell back. Grant tried, moved south.

And then I have stopped. I'm still,
breathing. The sun is on my face.
Birds warbling in the trees. My
lungs work. I'm still.

Says an officer: *General Grant, this is a crisis*
that cannot be looked upon too seriously.
I know Lee's methods well by past experience;
he will throw his whole army between us
and the Rapidan, and cut us off completely.

A long exhalation.

And Grant: *Oh, I am heartily tired of hearing*
about what Lee is going to do. Some of you always seem to think he is sud-
denly going to turn a double somersault,
and land in our rear and on both of our flanks at the same time.
Go back to your command, and try to think
what we are going to do ourselves,
instead of what Lee is going to do.

I wiggle my toes; they move.
My fingers, the same.
Slowly, carefully, I turn my head
to see my neighbor's house.

> Grant couldn't stand the sight
> of blood.

I push myself up onto my elbows.
The mower stands, two feet above me,
turned off by the dead man's switch.

> The northern papers called him a butcher.

I brush the dirt off. My shirt and shorts are
grass-stained. My hair has a little mud in it.

> The day after the two days, as the wounded
> burned, the Union Army assembled at a junction.
> Left went to the Rapidan; right, Richmond.
> Grant turned right.
> The soldiers cheered.

I stand up. What does it mean to get up
after falling down? What does it mean to continue
after injury?

> After the Wilderness, Grant and the Union Army
> marched south, to Spotsylvania Courthouse (18,000 casualties),
> to North Anna River (4,000), to Cold Harbor (13,000),
> to the siege at Petersburg and the surrender at Appomattox.

The body is a thing in motion in the universe.
Acted upon, acting upon. The mathematics of it and
all the outside forces boggle the mind.

The most popular man in America becomes president,
serves two full terms, fights for Reconstruction and reconciliation
but loses most of the South back to the Democrats,
loses most of his credibility by trusting unscrupulous men,
loses the family fortune in bad investments.

My body will fail again, fall again. Sometimes,
we call the parts of government bodies. It's imperfect,
this metaphor, but perhaps it helps us to understand
the fragility of the institution.

Sick with cancer, rushing to save his family from poverty,
Grant writes his memoirs, finishing them
and dying a few days later.
Of the Wilderness, he wrote: "More desperate fighting
has not been witnessed on this continent."

Our human bodies are fallible. The blood, the bones,
the muscle, the brain, all fragile, susceptible to
invasion and attack and injury. One day each will fail.
Yet we keep going forward, driven by grit and determination,
driven by our foolish sense of pride, driven by two things in
contradiction to one another. We make as many mistakes
as we win victories. We are desperately fighting.
We are fighting desperately. Those are different things.
Each propels us toward the goal in fits and starts,
on meandering roads and straightaways,
into reversals and dead ends. We stand up,
we brush off the dirt, we take stock of our dead.
We turn onto the road to our goal. We cheer.

Postcard Collection

Rutherford B. Hayes
Nineteenth President of the United States
1877-1881
90 years since the Constitution
14 years since the Emancipation
93 years until the resignation

1. "Fanny's Dollhouse"
An autopsy is the act of seeing with one's own eyes: auto-optics, self-sight. It is how we convince the dead to speak to us. We cut them open, pull them apart, weigh their organs like Anubis in the under-world, issue a report. We want inside. Little Fanny Hayes has two dollhouses, one made in 1877, the year her father took office, his election disputed until two days before inauguration; the other made by a Baltimore man in 1878. The postcard only shows their front façades, but we may imagine them opening up to reveal their interiors, revealing their secrets, giving us access to the domestic mind. And you have come to Spiegel Grove, home of Rutherford B. Hayes, for the same reason—to see inside the man by seeing inside his home, his library, his museum. You want inside.

2. "Gun Room"
He was wounded five times during the war, once through his left arm, breaking the bone. He had a horse shot out from under him, fought from Sumter to Appomattox. He preferred "General Hayes" to "Mister President," especially in retirement. On the tour of Spiegel Grove, what you learn is what the General accomplished, what the General liked, and very little about the President. By design, you imagine. A tour only lasts so long; a postcard from the gift shop only has so much space for a message.

3. "Sideboard w/China"
Large and mahogany, a bird and plant motif, carved at the request

of President and Mrs. Hayes in 1880, the year he tried to reform the patronage system of the Postal Service. But is this what you came to see? Fancy furniture? If so, please note the chair made out of bison horns in the entry hall of Spiegel Grove. In 1877, the Army chases the Nez Perce to Bear Paw, Montana, before they fight the Bannock in Idaho, before Hayes and Interior Secretary Schurz remove the Ponca to Indian Territory. The bison once covered the country. In the sideboard's mirror, you can see the case with Hayes's suit. Through his possessions, you see the man, but pull the metaphor's thread a little more: the suit is empty. The chair is empty. The autopsy empties out the body, weighs the organs, opens them up.

4. "Harrison Trail"
Hayes's uncle Sardis Birchard built the home, naming it Spiegel Grove for the pools of water that would form on the property after a storm. *Spiegel* is German for *mirror,* which suggests the place is given to reflection. But a photographer shoots a mirror from an angle, to remain invisible. To suggest an objectivity.

5. "Lover's Lane"
The house is lovely. The property is lovely. Wooded trails crisscross the twenty-five acres, and it all blends together in greenery. The Lover's Lane postcard is a vertically oriented version of the Harrison Trail postcard. When you visit, you will perhaps forget that you are in a small town in Ohio, and believe, as Sardis Birchard did, that this place might be from the fairy tales of your youth. When you visit, you might forget that the deal Hayes and the Republicans cut to resolve the 1876 election in their favor ended Reconstruction in the South, and that it took 132 years before an African-American returned to the Senate from the South.

6. "Hayes Home, Museum, & Library"
The gift shop, where you purchase your ticket to tour the home and museum, sells books and toys, plates and sweatshirts with Spiegel Grove on them. When you visit, they are making room for new postcards, and so the old postcards are bundled into plastic sandwich bags

and sold, nine for a dollar, as "Postcard Collection." Of the nine, not a single one shows a human being—no General Hayes, no Lucy, no Fanny, no Sardis, no one. Empty house, empty clothes, empty paths through the wooded estates. Don't forget that *souvenir* literally means *to remember.*

7. "Sardis Birchard's Bedroom"
Here we are, inside, the intimate places where the notable figures of history slept, sometimes where they died. What do the autopsy, the opened-up dollhouse, the picture postcard reveal about Hayes? What gets communicated from the past to the present and future in what we see with our own eyes? We visit a place, we take the tour, we look around, we buy a souvenir, we go on to the next stop.

8. "Lucy Hayes Reception Gown"
Let us have a moment for Lemonade Lucy, possibly the only First Lady people can name between Mary Todd Lincoln and Eleanor Roosevelt (alas, Lucretia Garfield! Alas, Lou Hoover!). There is the temperance stance, of course, but also the Easter Egg Roll on the White House lawn, which she began. She had eight children in an era when only five would live to adulthood, and when she died, the country's flags went to half-staff. On New Year's Day of 1878, she wore this gown to receive visitors, and now it is on display, empty, sleeves poised as if to grasp your hands in welcome.

9. "President Desk and Chair"
For less than four dollars, the United States Postal Service (founded by Benjamin Franklin, signed into law by George Washington, a reliable source of patronage jobs in the nineteenth century, and no longer a Cabinet Department as it was in Hayes's time, thanks to Nixon) will take these nine postcards and distribute them across the country, to Washington, DC, and Fremont, Ohio; to Indian Territory and the four other states that have joined the Union since Hayes left office after his promised single term; to the territories of the United States, including the Minor Outlying Islands; to the APOs of soldiers and

sailors fighting in our wars. The Postal Service will take all these small pieces of paper, with their photographs and words, almost anywhere you ask them to take them, and on them, you may write *We visited Spiegel Grove*. You may write *We saw Rutherford B. Hayes's things*. You may write *Wish you were here* or *I hope you are well* or *See you soon,* and then you will run out of room. But here is this: I wrote this in one place, and you are reading it with your own eyes in another, and perhaps that is insight enough for this autopsy, these photographs of a vacant chair, empty clothes, a desk with no papers.

American Still Life Paintings, 1820-1900: Gallery 69A

James Garfield
Twentieth President of the United States
1881
94 years since the Constitution
18 years since Emancipation
93 years until the resignation

Please, look:

I: Early Twentieth-Century Painting, c. 1900-1920: Gallery 71.

A train station once stood here. The Baltimore and Potomac Railroad stopped here, and so James Garfield stopped here, and was stopped here by an assassin who had bought a gun he thought would look good in a museum. The president's schedule was public. No need for concern in 1881; Lincoln and Booth had been the result of war passions sixteen years earlier. No need to worry. Nothing to watch out for.

So much for that. He's shot, lingers two and a half months, then dies in a house on the New Jersey shore. The train station lasts longer, then is gone too, in 1907. Later, Andrew Mellon, former Secretary of the Treasury and wealthy industrialist, builds the National Gallery of Art on the site.

All that's in the future, after the one thing anyone knows about President Garfield happens.

On view: George Bellows, *Both Members of This Club*, oil on canvas, 1909; Andrew Wyeth, *Wind from the Sea*, tempera on hardboard, 1947.

II: American Portraits, 1770-1845: Gallery 62.

Grew up poor. Grew up fatherless. Grew up the youngest, but did grow up, which counts for a lot. Drove mules for a while. Had the kind of childhood about which Horatio Alger wrote stories. Read a lot. Managed to go to school, leaving the mules behind. He later lamented the lack of a father figure.

On view: Edward Savage, *The Washington Family*, oil on canvas, c. 1790-1796; Thomas Sully, *The Coleman Sisters*, oil on canvas, 1844.

III: American Landscape and Genre Paintings, 1825-1865: Gallery 64.

He's from Ohio, no longer the wilderness but still the West in the eyes of the East. Born again at eighteen, dunked in an icy river, he lectures, teaches, preaches, works as a janitor—whatever lets him pursue his education. He studies in Massachusetts at Williams College—picture the rustic Ohioan among the East Coast's elite. Graduates salutatorian, returns to Ohio, becomes president of Hiram College, begins his move into politics. Then Lincoln, *The Union Is Dissolved*, and Fort Sumter.

On view: Asher Brown Durand, *Forest in the Morning Light*, oil on canvas, c. 1855; Durand, *Pastoral Landscape*, oil on canvas, 1861; Jasper Francis Cropsey, *The Spirit of War*, oil on canvas, 1851.

IV: Nineteenth-Century American Paintings: Gallery 65.

He's in the war, plays a supporting role in big battles—Shiloh and Chickamauga—and leads Union troops to victory under fire at the Battle of Middle Creek. He becomes a major general, sees the war as a holy crusade against slavery from its inception, and gets elected to Congress during the war—a seat he holds until he becomes president.

Garfield is the nineteenth century in America, even if he's only alive for half of it. Born rural and poor. Advances through education, religion, and the military. Participates in the defining conflict. On the right side of history, at least regarding slavery, from the start. We like these narratives. Horatio Alger wrote his campaign biography.

On view: George Henry Durrie, *Winter in the Country*, oil on canvas, c. 1859; Thomas Eakins, *Baby at Play*, oil on canvas, 1876; John Frederick Peto, *Take Your Choice*, oil on canvas, 1885.

V: American Landscapes, 1860-1885: Gallery 67.

He believes in gold. He believes in free trade. He believes in waving the bloody flag to remind the country of who started the war (Democrats), who killed their own brothers (Democrats), who held the slaves (Democrats), and who restored the Union (Republicans, especially radical Republicans like him). He's a little corrupt—there's a banking scandal and a salary raise, but they don't stick to him enough. He oversees the 1876 recount in Louisiana, where the election hangs in the balance. He is, officially, a neutral observer for Hayes and the Republicans, and he neutrally throws out a parish's votes, tipping the balance to Hayes, who wins by a single electoral vote. Four years later, Garfield wins the popular vote by fewer than 2,000. The electoral vote is not as close, but the Democrats still make rumbles about tampering.

On view: John La Farge, *The Last Valley—Paradise Rocks*, oil on canvas, 1867-1868; Frederic Edwin Church, *El Rio de Luz (The River of Light)*, oil on canvas, 1877; Sanford Robinson Gifford, *Ruins of the Parthenon*, oil on canvas, 1880.

VI: American Still-Life Paintings, 1820-1900: Gallery 69A.

Back where we began. Now everything freezes. Garfield's foot is poised, ready to step into the Baltimore and Potomac station on 6th Street, the Capitol in sight. A man with a gun prepares to step forward and take his shots. It always comes back to this, to trying to capture the ethereal, impossible, impossible. I am writing this essay on the Fourth of July in the National Gallery of Art's cafeteria, where I have paid two dollars and eighty-six cents for a cup of coffee. Around me, hundreds of people pass, enjoying the holiday, likely unaware that an American president, James Abram Garfield, was shot here in 1881 in a building that no longer exists. He was left-handed. He spoke Greek,

Latin, and Hebrew. His wife was named Lucretia, and they had seven children, and after he died, he was beloved enough that they put up a statue to him in front of the Capitol in Washington, not far from the train station where he was shot. He was crucial, he mattered, he was president of the United States, his assassination is as big of a *what if?* as Lincoln's or Kennedy's.

For some, time dims a life too quickly. It tries to convince us that none of it matters, none of it remains, all of it will be overshadowed by other events of history. We can try to paint a still-life, but the subject still just rots away in the end. We can put up a bronze statue of a man, and the environment around it will corrode it. We try, and we fail, and we forget, until the restoration comes, until they strip off the corrosion and lacquer and the grime of the years passing in order to remind us of what he once was, of what might have been.

On view: John Frederick Peto, *Still Life with Cake, Lemon, Strawberries, and Glass*, oil on canvas, 1890; Martin Johnson Heade, *Giant Magnolias on a Blue Velvet Cloth*, oil on canvas, c. 1890; Heade, *Still Life with Roses, Lilies, and Forget-Me-Nots in a Glass Vase*, oil on canvas, 1869.

Smear Campaign

Chester A. Arthur
Twenty-first President of the United States
1881-1885
94 years since the Constitution
18 years since Emancipation
89 years until the resignation

They say he was born in Canada. They say his grandfather was born in Ireland. They say he searched the records in Montréal to ensure there was no record of his birth. They say his grandfather's last name was MacArthur but he dropped the Mac to distance himself from the Roman Catholic (whispers: Irish, papist) side of his family. They say his associates in Canada called his father "Billy" Arthur. They say the son born to Billy Arthur, named Chester Alan Arthur, was born in Dunham Flats, Quebec, Canada, and they say he cannot be fit for the office of the vice president because of the Twelfth Amendment, and God help us if Garfield dies and Arthur becomes president.

Where's the birth certificate? They said that Frémont was a Catholic. They said that Jefferson had mixed blood. They said that Jackson was a bigamist. They say they say they say. We've heard candidates called bigots and secret Muslims, seen fake news, seen them swift-boated, seen their hopes go down the river, the neat calligraphy of a campaign smeared across the page. You have to get dirty to win. Don't you?

They say *He never knew the smell of gunpowder.* They say he enriched his friends while Quartermaster of the Union Army, while he was Collector of the Port of New York. They say he was corrupt to the core. They say Garfield was against the patronage jobs, the star routes of the postal service, the ripe plums handed out to the electoral winners, but Arthur? They say Arthur was rotten. And then Guiteau shoots Garfield and surrenders to the authorities, saying *I am a stalwart of the Stalwarts—Arthur is president now!*

They say Garfield is dying in a town by the beach. Arthur, in his townhouse in Manhattan, doesn't believe it, doesn't want to believe it, wants the cup taken away, but the telegram comes anyway. They find a New York Supreme Court justice, a man named Brady, to administer the oath—*execute the office*—in the parlor.

Hold your breath as Garfield dies in New Jersey. They say they could have saved him if the doctors hadn't infected him with their unwashed hands, their unsterilized instruments. Hold your breath, because they say Arthur will gather up all the spoils of the system to give to his cronies.

The telegram arrives, then Brady arrives, then Arthur says the oath—*solemnly swear, best of my ability*—and now, in a room full of men on Lexington Avenue in 1881, he is president. Feel free to imagine a moment of silence.

Then the work begins, and he surprises everyone. He is not corrupt, even if he had once been. He does not give patronage jobs to cronies. He orders prosecution of the postal service's patronage regardless of party affiliation. He expertly wields the veto to deny Congress their overreaching. He refuses to sign a bill banning Chinese immigration for twenty years, calling the length of the ban *a breach of our national faith* for its exclusion of an entire generation. He vetoes a bill to improve rivers and harbors because they only improve the nearby towns and are thus *not for the common defense or general welfare*, he says, quoting the Constitution.

But smear him appropriately: he signs a revision of the bill that excludes the Chinese from the country for ten years, the first time this country closes its borders to a group. This is a stain, a large one, on him. Yet there is something to say about President Arthur besides the fact of his presidency, how he is one of the few dozen men to hold the office, even if it seems as though that might be all anyone remembers about him. You may visit New York City, and walk down Lexington Avenue to number 123, and stand in front of the Indian market on the ground floor of that building, the other place in our nation's first capital where a president took the oath of office. Washington stood in Federal Hall, and Arthur stood here. You may try to read the plaque marking the occasion, but the Plexiglas that protects it is smeared with the dirt of the city and barely allows for legibility. And you may say something about President Arthur to the people walking past you, but they walk so quickly and they speak so loudly in their one hundred languages—English and Spanish and French and Swahili and Hindi and Malay and, of course, Chinese—that everything you say, everything they say, everything we say will combine into its own American language, a language of today and tomorrow, a language floating up to the sky, past the window of the parlor in which, long ago, he said the oath.

Never Odd

Grover Cleveland
Twenty-second President of the United States
1885-1889
98 years since the Constitution
22 years since the Emancipation
85 years until the resignation

Let us do right by you, Grover Cleveland: such a meteoric rise, just four years from lawyer to mayor to governor to president. That is a kind of story that America loves to tell—the idea that anyone who works hard will be a success. When you begin your term, what the American people want is for you to keep your campaign promises—the lure of prosperity, the fight against corruption, the primacy of gold and only gold. They expect these things of you, first Democrat in office since the Civil War. And you'll use the office to do the job; you'll lower the trade tariff, reduce silver coinage, civilize the Indian by breaking their common land into individual plots—

out of one, many. You'll
wield the veto like soldiers
did bayonets in the war you
paid another man to fight—
accepted practice then, but
the voters who did fight at
Shiloh and Gettysburg don't
forgive. When you veto bills
to grant more pensions, when
you return the South's battle
flags (those hard-won tro-
phies soaked with northern
blood), these men will remember, and when you stand
for re-election, you'll lose the
northern states because those
veterans will not vote for you.
It's not all sadness and conflict in this term. You'll marry in the White House. You'll
name two justices to the Supreme Court. Even when you
lose, you still win the popular
vote (shades of Quincy Adams, shades of Tilden, predecessor of Gore and Clinton).
Still: you lose. One supposes
the appropriate thing to do
is retire from public life. You
know differently. You have
plans. When you move out,
your wife tells the staff *We
are coming back four years from
today*, so leave the furnishings
as they are, keep them clean,

make sure that Harrison and his family don't ruin them—you'll need them when you return.

A Brief Interlude in Which We May Contemplate the Unknowability of Benjamin Harrison, President of the United States, 1889-1893

Benjamin Harrison
Twenty-third President of the United States
1889-1893
102 years since the Constitution
26 years since Emancipation
81 years until the resignation

Here's your pivot point, a new recorded history, an invisible man, a few seconds of sound, his voice scratchy on the Edison cylinder recording the speech: *As president of the United States, I was present at the first Pan-American congress in Washington, DC. I believe that with God's help, our two countries shall continue to live side-by-side in peace and prosperity.* Then his name: *Benjamin Harrison.*

What *Pan-American?* What *Washington?* What *Harrison?* What happened there? What other country? Who's recording the speech? Who's writing the entries?

A set of books used to be the technology by which you discovered knowledge; take the *H* volume off the shelf, find him and his presidential grandfather listed between *Harrisburg* and *Harrow,* and learn about him. Today, all you have to do is to type the sixteen letters of his name into a search field, and your first result will be his Wikipedia entry, tended by volunteer editors (Harrison knew volunteers, led them through the Civil War) who mostly make minute adjustments to his entry, capitalizing "Civil War" or reverting earlier edits or leaving notes like *Past-perfect tense seems a little bit better here,* making sure the entry is clean and accurate, like families sweeping a tombstone on Memorial Day. This is how most of us learn about Benjamin Harrison now.

You can click through the edit history of his entry and watch the memory of him slowly be built. First the fact of his existence and presidency, then the name of his vice president (Levi Morton), then links to the two elections (1888, victory; 1892, defeat), then the first biography of him—or rather, links to his great-grandfather of the same name, father of William Henry Harrison, another less-known chief executive, tacked onto the bottom of the page for disambiguation purposes. Four months after that entry, his own biography—senator from Indiana, Civil War general, First Lady named Caroline—appears to accompany it.

Harrison was the only son of Indiana to become president, although he was surrounded, like some strange joke of the Midwest, by Cleveland—Grover, not Ohio. Harrison served one term and is mostly remembered as a caretaker president.

If we comb through the edits, though, we see more about Harrison, more beyond caretaker. He added six western states to the Union, vastly increasing the size of the country. He quintupled the number of warships in the navy and had the White House wired for electricity. And he is the first president whose voice we can hear, the real thing, underneath the staticky crackles of the wax cylinder, and only for thirty-six seconds, but it is the man himself, frozen for a half-minute in history.

Who edits as time moves him away? His body remains in a cemetery called Crown Hill, like some strange joke about monarchy and caretaker presidents. His voice is fixed, first on wax, then on magnetic tape, now in MP3—a fitting legacy for a president invested in technology. An army of volunteers keeps editing his entry, fixing this and changing that, doing and undoing edits, listening for him in the static for the sounds, adjusting the signal-to-noise ratio, turning the cylinder over and over to find the man inside.

Or Even

Grover Cleveland
Twenty-fourth President of the United States
1893-1897
106 years since the Constitution
30 years since the Emancipation
77 years until the resignation

When you return, the first thing to do is reverse the doings of Harrison, to repair the things he ruined. You and Frances, new daughter Ruth (she of candy-bar fame) in tow, are back in the White House, pulling off the incredible—a second term served nonconsecutively. Never before. Never again. (Now the appropriate thing to do is retire). You undo the move toward silver. You undo the higher tariffs (shades of Taft, of Wilson). You name two Supreme Court justices, although this time the Senate fights you, hard. There's a lot of sadness and conflict. There's a financial panic early in your term and a railroad strike you'll try to break by using the army and navy

to ensure the mail will go
through. An army of men
will march on Washington to
demand jobs, and although
they'll scatter when they
reach the Capitol, the voters will remember the man
who lost the common touch.
And then the businessmen in
Hawaii who overthrow the
queen—that's your problem
too. So is your own body,
cancer in your jaw, a secret
surgery on board the presidential yacht. Your face will
change, rebuilt by prosthet-
ics. You'll try to use the office
to do the job, but everything
runs against you—the trains,
the businessmen, the body,
and finally your own party,
run by silverites, nominating another man, who'll lose
over and over. You're the last
Democrat in office until the
one who oversees the Great
War. Grover Cleveland,
the promises you tried to
keep: prosperity, corruption,
gold—they don't matter. Everything is so much different from when you began;
such a precipitous fall, from
president to private citizen,
repudiated by your party, but

then again, you land on your feet (a beloved ending to an American story), retiring to Princeton. Elected, defeated, elected, repudiated, and just before your death, you say "I have tried so hard to do right."

Assassin's Bullet

William McKinley
Twenty-fifth President of the United States
1897-1901
110 years since the Constitution
34 years since Emancipation
73 years until the resignation

I. The organist starts to play Schumann's "Träumerei," the center-piece of the thirteen sections of *Kinderszenen* (*Scenes from Childhood*). The president continues shaking hands. A man reaches out, his right hand wrapped in a handkerchief. His hand is on fire. His name is unspeakable.

They are in Buffalo, not far from Niagara Falls and Canada. They are practically on the border. The man with the hand of fire is from Detroit, the son of Polish immigrants. His name is difficult. Say it: *sawz-logz.* Say it: *chawl-gosh.* Say it: *zal-gotz.*

II. William McKinley, by many accounts, was a friendly man. He was shaking the hands of visitors to the Pan-American Exhibition of 1901 in Buffalo when an assassin approached him and shot him twice. For eight days, McKinley hovered on the edge of life and death before dying just two hours into the morning of September 14, 1901.

Death is a public thing at this time in American history, a com-monplace occurrence. Mourners would drape the pictures of the dece-dent with black cloth, the women would wear black veils, the clocks stopped at the moment of death. Rather than be buried at home, the decedent would likely be buried in a parklike cemetery, where mourn-ers would leave flowers on their grave. They would make souvenirs from the hair of the decedent, wreathes and rings and other pieces by which they might never forget the dead, and by which the rest of the world might know their acts of remembrance, their ceremonies for the lost.

III. At the 1901 Pan-American Exposition in Buffalo, an x-ray machine, a new technology, is on display. None of the doctors can find the bullet lodged in President William McKinley. The x-ray machine stands unused.

IV. The Secret Service has only begun protecting the president seven years earlier. McKinley's secretary, George B. Cortelyou, asks McKinley not to attend the reception at the Temple of Music, as such events pose a security risk.

"Why should I? No one would wish to hurt me," says the president.

V. In the Smithsonian Museum of American History, a 1900 campaign poster shows McKinley standing atop a giant gold coin held up by farmers in suspenders, bow-tied businessmen, and sailors. PROSPERITY AT HOME, it reads. PRESTIGE ABROAD. The candidate holds an American flag in one hand, doffs his top hat with the other. COMMERCE. CIVILIZATION. There are sailing ships and smokestacks. Behind it all, a sun, undoubtedly rising.

We forget that most presidents served single terms. In the nineteenth century, only seven presidents won re-election to a consecutive second term. When McKinley runs for his second term in 1900, it is under the slogan "Four More Years of the Full Dinner Pail." America is content, will continue going in the direction of the sunrise. McKinley is re-elected by almost a million more votes than his Democratic rival, William Jennings Bryan.

VI. By the time of McKinley's assassination, four other presidents have died in office: Harrison, Taylor, Lincoln, and Garfield, the last two also by the bullet. People begin to notice a pattern: Harrison elected in 1840, Lincoln 1860, Garfield 1880, and now McKinley, winner in 1900. Harding, Roosevelt, Kennedy will follow; people say each man is a victim of the Curse of Tecumseh, the Shawnee leader killed by Harrison in 1813 during the War of 1812. Reagan is shot in 1981 but survives, the curse broken.

VII. The word *assassin* has its origin in the Arabic *hashishin*, "hashish eaters," referring, according to the Oxford English Dictionary, "to the Ismaili sectarians, who used to intoxicate themselves with hashish or hemp, when preparing to dispatch some king or public man."

Leon Czolgosz, the man who shot William McKinley, was electrocuted. *The New York Times* wrote:

> As he was being seated he looked about at the assembled witnesses with quite a steady stare and said: "I killed the president because he was an enemy of the good people — of the working people."
>
> His voice trembled slightly at first, but gained strength with each word, and he spoke perfect English.
>
> "I am not sorry for my crime,' he said loudly, just as the guard pushed his head back on the rubber headrest and drew the strap across his forehead and chin."
>
> Then, as calm as he could be, Czolgosz was electrocuted. The *Times* reported that his body strained so hard against the chair that the arms "creaked perceptibly."

A photo of Czolgosz taken while he awaited his death shows him staring through the latticed bars of his cell, hands to either side of his head, staring, staring, staring. His eyes are nothing, all interior, all dreaming, waiting for the ritual and ceremony that will end his time on Earth.

VIII. McKinley did not die immediately. Doctors operated on him in the emergency hospital at the Pan-American Exposition, a temporary facility lacking any electrical lighting. As the sun set, a doctor used a mirror to focus the sun's rays on McKinley. Candles could not be lit because of the flammable ether used to sedate the president.

After the surgery, McKinley was moved to the house of the Exposition's director. He regained consciousness, spoke to doctors and his wife, ate a little. Vice president Theodore Roosevelt returned to his mountain retreat. Mark Hanna, the president's campaign manager, said the president might be able to return home soon.

IX. Czolgosz was an anarchist, part of that wave of anarchists that had felled other world leaders: Empress Elisabeth of Austria, King

Umberto I of Italy, President Carnot of France, Shah Nasser al-Din of Persia, Czar Alexander II of Russia, more. An anarchist's bullet would push the world to war thirteen years later.

But in America, nothing. Roosevelt became president upon the death of McKinley. The government continued, unbroken.

X. Assassination marked McKinley. If he is known today, recognized at any level beyond his name and his title, it is the manner of his death, the way that a man who had wrapped a gun in a handkerchief shot him twice in Buffalo. His death overshadows the life. He had driven rations under fire to starving Union troops at the Battle of Antietam; he was the last of the Civil War veterans to become president. He led the country through the Spanish-American War. He was the last president of the nineteenth century and the first of the twentieth.

Among other things, he has become two bullets, and one of those rolled out of his jacket when he was undressed for surgery. One bullet, then, fired from a gun bought for $4.50, wrapped in a handkerchief. Assassins' tools are simple, but their effects are remarkable: they end their victims' lives.

XI. Thomas Edison made a film recreating the execution of the anarchist, releasing it about six months after the assassination. It runs about four minutes, the first of which shows a panoramic view of the exterior of Auburn Prison. An interior shot: four guards walk to the anarchist's cell and take him out, leading him to the electric chair. They strap him down, tie a black band across his eyes. Then the warden gives the signal, and the anarchist strains once, twice, three times against the restraints (remember: *creaked perceptibly*; you'll hear it on the soundtrack of Edison's silent film, you'll imagine that terribleness). Then the prison doctor places a stethoscope against the anarchist's chest. The warden nods, to confirm the death. Then the movie ends.

XII. McKinley deteriorated on the seventh day, Friday, September 13, 1901. The track of the bullet that had entered his abdomen, the one that could not be found, turned gangrenous. Cortelyou, still by the president's side, called friends and officials to his bedside.

"It is useless, gentlemen," said McKinley. "I think we ought to have prayer."

Late in the day, his wife arrived and came to his bedside. McKinley had taken care of her for decades. Now she will outlive him. Assassination makes things into the things they should not be; the healthy, dead; the free, imprisoned; the ship of state set to sail without its captain.

"Goodbye, goodbye all. It is God's way. His will, not ours, be done." Then he said, as best he could, the words to his favorite hymn, "Nearer My God to Thee." The Confederate Army band played the song as the survivors of Pickett's Charge limped back across the fields of Gettysburg. It's played at Garfield's funeral; it will be played at Ford's funeral. They'll play it on the *Titanic* in eleven years. In America, the song is sung to the tune of "Bethany," written by the same man who wrote "Mary Had a Little Lamb."

"Nearer my God to thee," whispered McKinley, and then he was through speaking. A little after two o'clock that night, Dr. Rixey placed a stethoscope against the president's chest, and brought the ceremony to a close.

bully

Theodore Roosevelt
Twenty-sixth President of the United States
1901-1909
114 years since the Constitution
38 years since Emancipation
65 years until the resignation

they call him *teedie* as a boy, as the weak boy shut up in the family's
brownstone on twentieth street *teedie roosevelt,* shut in the brownstone,
the gilded cage, the volume of j p wood's *natural history* his way out,
words and pictures in the low light of a stormy manhattan afternoon
what aggravates his lungs: excitement, exertion, strain, the things the
industrialized and natural worlds outside his windows share in common, could provide to him if he could only catch his breath; if only his
small lungs did not seize they tell him he can never be out he can never be in the world   when he cannot breathe his father
is the one who can best convince his lungs to unclench their fists to
calm the fight to bring peace, his father the philanthropist, the good
man, the man who taught his son that he would not tolerate *selfishness
or cruelty, idleness, cowardice, or untruthfulness* but the father also the man
who paid another man to take his place in the war the son's shame at
this   but the father still the man against the doctors encourages
him to exercise to break asthma's grip on him, then boxing and wrestling and hiking and everything else   and from the father the
idea takes root in him of power and kindness—that the weakness
inside him can be overcome through work if he can work harder than
everyone else then he cannot fail and then the willingness to take up
the fight in all the ways yes the rough riders yes san juan hill yes the
great white fleet yes big-stick diplomacy but also the fight in america
so trust-busting so a minimum guaranteed wage so a pure food and
drug act so inviting booker t washington to dinner at the white house

the first black man to dine there as a guest the southern democrats enraged but theodore will not be bullied will not stop the fight the breathless rush of change and excitement in the opening years of the twentieth century   even the safari to africa after leaving office because the violence of hunting leads to the strength of education decades after reading j p wood on twentieth street he helps fill the smithsonian's new natural history museum   even his speeches a staccato blast in his surprisingly gentle voice a voice combining both the refined and the natural harvard and the outdoors the rules and the breaking of the rules   he's president because his enemies stick him in the least powerful position in america the vice presidency but then czolgosz and mckinley meet so then kindness: he inherits almost a full term elected again on his own so he will not seek a second elected term a third term really and instead his friend taft ascends to the office   and strength four years later because his friend *means well but he means well feebly* and this is not a place for the weak to lead when he loses he saves himself through work sending himself down a tributary of the amazon the river of doubt and survives what should have killed most other men, the illness the injury the river the natives who debate nightly about killing the white men in their midst and decide not to kill, the mercy of strength   i do not mean to praise him or his strength or to suggest he is without flaw he is with flaw or to argue that combat is our first route to success because that has not been america's story these days or my story or perhaps not your story but there is something in the striving that i admire something in the desire to gain power so that it might be used well for the less fortunate   that seems like the best impulse of this country because either a constitution written by white landowning males has malfunctioned because it has expanded its rights to people they did not or could not conceive of as human   or it has functioned exactly the way they meant it to function, unclenching the freedoms it took violently, letting them expand, letting them breathe, letting the air of liberty rush into the lungs   *teedie* becomes *teddy* becomes *Theodore*   he dies at night asleep his lungs of course one son ahead of him in the darkness shot down over germany in the war to end war

and another son telegraphing the remaining siblings *the old lion is dead*
i don't know if i believe the metaphor of president-as-father but it
seems fair to ask what did they give when they walked the halls with
us as our lungs seized and we gasped for breath?   the fight?
the peace?

Judgment

William H. Taft
Twenty-seventh President of the United States
1909-1913
122 years since the Constitution
46 years since Emancipation
61 years until the resignation

Bench: "On days that opinions are announced by the Court from the bench, the text of each opinion is made available immediately to the public and press in a printed form called a 'bench opinion.'" —"Information About Opinions," supremecourt.gov

If you know anything about William Howard Taft, it's probably his weight. He did get stuck in the White House bathtub; that's not a legend. Maybe you know the story that his presidency so disappointed Theodore Roosevelt (his mentor, who had chosen him as his successor) that Roosevelt ran against him in the next election. Maybe you know that he joined the Supreme Court after the presidency, but that already feels like pushing the boundaries of common knowledge.

Slip: "Several days after an opinion is announced by the Court, it is printed in a 6" x 9" self-cover pamphlet called a 'slip opinion' . . . in the case of discrepancies between the bench and slip opinions, the slip opinion controls."—"Information About Opinions"

He was a man with a legal mind, and his early days show a man setting himself toward the bench. Attended Yale, Skull and Bones, Linonian Society. Secrecy and debate. He wrestled too, as big men often do, and as big men often do, he understood how his body worked. He could dance, could negotiate spaces around him. Power and grace—that sort of thing. And the career moves steadily forward—judge of the Superior Court of Cincinnati, then the Harrison administration's solicitor

86

general, the youngest ever at just thirty-two years old, the lawyer who stands in front of the Supreme Court on the government's behalf, in the chambers of Congress where the Court meets, as it has no home of its own. Then the Court of Appeals, and a professor of constitutional law at Cincinnati—he is moving up. He is an Ohio Republican when being an Ohio Republican means entry into the halls of power.

It's not fair, our reduction of him. But how else do we judge a man? The complexity of the question is impossible, like trying to imagine how a man might fall upwards.

Preliminary Print: "The preliminary prints of the U.S. Reports are the third generation of opinion publication and dissemination. These are brown, self-cover 'advance pamphlets' that contain, in addition to the opinions themselves, all of the announcements, tables, indexes, and other features that make up the U. S. Report . . . in case of discrepancies between the slip opinion and preliminary print version of a case, the preliminary print controls." —"Information About Opinions"

What changes our minds? How do we form opinions? How do we decide? President McKinley, an Ohio Republican, asks Taft to govern the new American territory of the Philippines, to leave the judgment of the law to foster its execution. Taft had opposed annexation, and McKinley knows his ambition is for the Supreme Court, but Taft says yes. His commitment to his decision is such that when, three years later, Roosevelt offers him an associate justice's seat on the Court, Taft turns it down, because in his opinion the Philippines cannot yet govern themselves.

Ambitions at play: Roosevelt, who sees Taft as a trusted figure, one he names Secretary of War and grooms for the presidency; Helen Taft, politically ambitious in a time when women cannot vote, who pushes her husband further into politics; and Taft himself, who knows that what he really wants is not any seat on the Supreme Court, but *the* seat on the Court. He is aimed for Chief Justice, and he will find his way there somehow.

He runs for president, reluctantly, but how can he say no to Roosevelt when he could not say no to McKinley? He is the party's available man. But as president, he falters. He cannot charm the press or the public, as Roosevelt could do so masterfully. Devotion to the law and precedent makes being a Progressive difficult. Yet he files anti-trust lawsuits and submits the first modern presidential budget. He is president when a Constitutional amendment creates the federal income tax. He makes changes that endure. Not enough. His friend Roosevelt turns on him, forming a third party, and the vote is split, and the Democrat, Wilson, a southerner relocated to New Jersey, becomes president.

So he's done. We can close the books on him. Starting in 1948, surveys of both historians and the public rank him near the middle: not good, not bad. Impartial. He leaves, loses weight (stress and worry make a man eat), and we can suppose that's all.

Then, in 1921, Edward Douglass White, Chief Justice of the Supreme Court, dies. The president, Warren G. Harding, is an Ohio Republican.

Bound: "The fourth and final generation of opinion publication is the casebound set of law books entitled United States Reports. The opinions and other materials contained in the preliminary prints are republished in this series of books . . . in case of discrepancies between the preliminary print and bound volume versions of a case, the bound volume controls." —"Information About Opinions"

Justice Frankfurter tells Justice Brandeis that he cannot understand "why a man who is so good as chief justice . . . could have been so bad as president." But we can speculate, can talk about a devotion to law, an ambitious wife, an overpowering boss, a tendency to say yes when he should say no, a tendency to say no when he should say yes, and maybe generously, a foresight to see a winding path to his ultimate goal—after all, he was the one who appointed the aged White to the Chief Justice's seat. He understood legacy. In 1929, as Chief Justice, he convinces Congress to build the Court its own home, a permanent building for the bench. As a young man, he stood on one side.

A presidency later, he sat on the other. There is one room in which the Supreme Court has met since Taft's building was dedicated, five years after he died, and it is where the twentieth century was shaped, where the twenty-first century is being shaped. There is one bench and nine seats, one podium from which every case is argued—*Brown vs. Board, Roe vs. Wade, Bush vs. Gore, Citizens United vs. Federal Election Commission, Obergefell vs. Hodges*, all of them, spoken and argued and judged in a space made possible by Taft, a man who found a way for a former president to surpass his office.

All Good Men

Woodrow Wilson
Twenty-eighth President of the United States
1913-1921
126 years since the Constitution
50 years since Emancipation
53 years until the resignation

In 1919, a small vessel in Woodrow Wilson's brain burst, whether overtaxed by the Great War or the Treaty of Versailles or the failure of the United States to join his League of Nations. That small vessel burst, and the three pounds inside his skull changed. To put it lightly.

He had given three speeches a day, every day, traveling around the country, trying to save the peace he had put into motion. Over and over, the same speech, the endless parade of citizens, the train rattling from site to site, his brain, his delicate brain, his professor's brain, his Princeton brain working and working and working.

In hindsight, of course something would give. In Colorado, he collapsed; a week later, in the White House, the vessel burst and the stroke hit him. It was, as the doctors say, massive. To put it bluntly.

The brain is what the president needs. That capacity for rational thought in crisis, out of crisis, in war and in peace—it is so crucial, so absolutely necessary. The external pressures upon it are greater than we imagine, and so, again, the terrible logic of Wilson's stroke.

Look at any president at the start and again at the end of his term, observe the slow deterioration, the gray hair, the deeply etched wrinkles, the slumped-down posture. Consider the way they are invigorated at their successor's inauguration (think of Buchanan telling Lincoln in the carriage on the way to the Capitol *If you are as happy in entering the White House as I shall feel on returning to Wheatland you are a happy man*). Every year takes the toll of two years, of three years. One term is difficult; two terms seem impossible. FDR made it through three, but it makes a terrible logic that his brain hemorrhaged at the beginning of his fourth. It killed him in minutes, but to be honest, it had been killing him all along. This job murders men.

Impossible to imagine in a twenty-four-hour news cycle, but Wilson vanishes from the public eye, while parts of himself also begin to disappear: his vision in his right eye, the movement on the left side of his body. These things are connected, the body's wires crossing between the head and the hands.

His wife, Edith, runs things. She sends instructions to the Cabinet and restricts access to Wilson. She makes decisions about the railroads and Cabinet members, and with the help of an aide and a journalist, she manufactures an "interview" with Wilson to prove his capacity to lead even as he convalesces. She is, to put it clearly, the acting president.

As they courted, in the wake of the death of Wilson's first wife, Wilson brought Edith into his world. He mailed her packets of documents, asking for her thoughts on them. During the war, they would decode messages together. He respected her mind, and she, in turn, his, announcing after his stroke that his "brain was clear and untouched," even if she was the only person to believe so.

What she does is enough. It gets him to the end of his second term, to retirement in the Kalorama neighborhood of Washington. He has an elevator in the house. He has a collection of canes given to him by friends and dignitaries (once the secret is out, of course). He has a typewriter, and his hands fit on the home row.

One is strong, as powerful as it ever was. The other, enfeebled, cannot press the keys. The left hand is gone, the recognizable letters of his name: WDRW. The right gives us only a moan: OOO. With a stretch, he may type the name of his love, the woman who ran the country: EDTH.

Similarly, we may type the simple facts of his presidency. Woodrow Wilson was president of Princeton, governor of New Jersey. He served two terms. He kept the country out of war, then he led it through the Great War. With one hand, we might note that women gained the vote during his presidency. With our other hand, we could record that he had no problem with segregation and enshrined it in the federal government for decades to follow. We may write down trivia: he promised voters a "New Freedom" platform; he founded the Federal Reserve System, which is why he is on the one-hundred-thousand-dollar bill, which is no longer in circulation. (*Reserve* is a word that can be typed by the left hand alone.) He suffered a stroke, but he lived, and he outlived the man who succeeded him to office. Eventually all these things become history, or trivia, or filler on a page: now is the time for all good men to come to the aid of their country; the quick brown fox jumped over the lazy dogs; lorem ipsum.

Woodrow Wilson's brain killed him in 1924 with another stroke. His wife, Edith, who once ran the country, lived another thirty-seven years, and she died the day the Woodrow Wilson Bridge over the Potomac River opened, a bridge that crosses from Virginia through a small corner of the District of Columbia to Maryland, connecting people and places. Traffic on the bridge is often heavy, and when the cars are stopped over the water, drivers can look to the north and see the Washington Monument but not the Woodrow Wilson Memorial, which is less than a half-mile away, a relief sculpture of his head hidden inside another building named for another president, who also died of a brain disease, although not the same one as Wilson.

Perhaps Wilson taxes our own brains too much, to the point of exhaustion rather than destruction. We do not know whether to consign him to the dustbin of history for his outmoded and offensive ways of thinking or commemorate him for his idealism and globalism. Perhaps we should think on it a little longer, as though we were figuring a complex mathematical problem. Perhaps we could consider the obelisk we dedicated to Washington and its height, and whether, as the sun sets in the west, its cast shadow might ever touch the head of Woodrow Wilson.

The Smoke-Filled Room

Warren G. Harding
Twenty-ninth President of the United States
1921-1923
134 years since the Constitution
58 years since Emancipation
51 years until the resignation

It's all out of your hands now.

From a room in Chicago's Blackstone Hotel, the decision comes forth. You, Warren G. Harding, Ohio's son: you will be the candidate; you will be the president.

The cigars burn in the smoke-filled room. You can see the embers glow, the cherries, they're called. The party bosses regard you. They ask you if there's anything lurking in the closet. Anything they should know. You think of Florence, your wife. You think of Nan, your mistress. The other girls.

No, you say. It's your one moment of agency, that lie. That's all. Nothing else.

The men in the smoke-filled room nod. You are now the candidate, and with the next ballot of the convention, the tenth, the stalemate breaks. Florence, your wife, is so surprised she accidentally jabs your political manager with a hatpin.

The managers. You are managed. Your job for the campaign is to give speeches from your front porch. The managers will do the rest.

They'll film you (new technology) and send the footage to the newsreels.

They'll bring celebrities (new tactics) to the front porch and photograph you with them, eight thousand photos of you and Florence every two weeks.

They'll train speakers to go around the country and talk to people about you. Five thousand speakers, two thousand of them female (new voting block).

They'll telephone people (new technology) at their homes, call them, tell them *Vote for Harding*, tell them *Return to normalcy*.

They'll help them forget the war, Mr. Wilson's war, *over there*, the trenches, the gas, the boys who didn't come home, the ones who did, shell-shocked, faces and bodies destroyed. That's all over for the public. You're the man, they say, to return us to normalcy.

You'll never go back to normalcy. When you step off the wood of that porch to go to Washington, your feet will never touch it again.

Your image is out of your hands. Your voice on the recordings is out of your hands. You're elected. The men in the smoke-filled room take over.

They make the decisions. They issue the contracts. They find a little place called Teapot Dome and make it a synonym for scandal, make it the reason the House can demand officials' tax returns from the IRS. They take the Justice Department and the Shipping Board and fill their own coffers from them. (The Veterans Bureau, too, so soon after the war, with all those veterans to help.)

They're a gang. You're nothing. You live in the White House. They meet in a green house on K Street and plan their riches. From the Blackstone Hotel to here. From the Blackstone Hotel to there.

You say to William Allen White, *I have no trouble with my enemies, but my damn friends, they're the ones that keep me walking the floor nights!*

It's the most famous thing you say.

Passive voice, Warren G. Harding. You are done to. You are undone. You are literally the second person, the one not in charge, the one removed. You are lost in this place, this smoke-filled room, this White House, this executive mansion, this prison.

But you know enough to know that in America, you go west to escape.

Ohio was once the frontier, your front porch a wilderness. So you go west.

First to Saint Louis, then Kansas, Denver, Tacoma. Then to Alaska and Canada, the first president to do so. You give a speech to fifty thousand in Vancouver, amplified by microphones (new technology).

You are far from the front porch, from the smoke-filled room.

Are you your own man? You are weaker without them, without the men in the smoke-filled room. Never forget: they are the doers. You are done to.

You are done for.

In San Francisco, your heart gives out. In the terror of it, in the shooting pains down the left arm that no one pays attention to, in the misdiagnosis a week earlier of food poisoning, in those final moments of your life, a life of affability and malleability, do you feel the smallest bit of relief?

Today, the surveys of historians rank you near the bottom. You, Nixon, Grant, Andrew Johnson. The corruptible. It may not be your fault. You were, if nothing else, a pleasant man, someone with whom to pass the time on the front porch. You had friends you trusted.

Relief seems a ridiculous notion. Perhaps in those final moments in the hotel room in San Francisco, you thought of Florence, of Nan, of new technology, of new tactics, of the future. Maybe you thought of the moment when they brought you into the smoke-filled room, the moment before the moment that mattered, and asked you about yourself.

Go ahead, imagine it: a moment in which you might have told the men why you should not be the nominee, a moment in which you stop the corruption before it goes any further, a moment in which you said *yes. I have secrets.*

They cannot be taken from me.

Silence

Calvin Coolidge
Thirtieth President of the United States
1923-1929
136 years since the Constitution
60 years since Emancipation
45 years until the resignation

There's this story about Calvin Coolidge—maybe you've heard it?—in which these two women approach him and one says, "I have bet my friend that I can get you to say three words," and the famously taciturn president says only, "You lose."

The beginning of the presidency is an act of speech. In a cold month, Americans gather on the lawn of the National Mall and watch the new president place his hand on a book, raise the other, and take the oath of office by speaking the words written in the Constitution out loud.

What the president says matters, the speeches they give, the round tables and debates and town halls, even their tweets, all carry more gravity than that of ordinary civilians. What are we to make of Calvin Coolidge, a quiet man, Silent Cal, a president remembered not for his stirring orations but instead his lack thereof?

There's this story about Coolidge, about when he became president. He was visiting at the family farm in Vermont, and in the middle of the night, a messenger arrived, informing the vice president that President Harding had died in California, and now Coolidge would become the president. Coolidge dressed and then took the oath of office by kerosene lamp in the family parlor, administered by his father, a justice of the peace. Then, the story goes, he went back to sleep, his term begun with the speech act, words that change the state of being.

Can you imitate the president's voice? Can you move your arms

96

the way he does, mimic the verbal tics, follow the cadence of his speech? Washington was apparently very quiet; Lincoln's voice was high-pitched, and when he became more agitated, his arms would flap up and down. Think of the places their voices suggest—Massachusetts and Texas and Georgia and Arkansas. Think of how the vowels round in the mouth, how the breath might draw out an A or a tongue might snap a T.

It's easier now. We see the president more often, hear his voice daily. We have models for our imitations, actors who recreate him on comedy shows. Sometimes we imitate the impressions instead of the real thing, our imitations a game of telephone, of diminishing returns.

There's this story about Coolidge that my father told me: that he was a distant relative of ours. I don't know if it's a true story. I don't see the connection between his Vermont Congregationalists and our Iowa Catholics. I also don't see why my father would lie about this—what caché could we gain from being related to Coolidge? Maybe it's a story I've told myself. Maybe no one ever told the story.

The president says words, starting with the oath of office, then the inaugural address. He addresses Congress from time to time, as required by the Constitution, to discuss the state of the Union. Perhaps he delivers a farewell address. He could deliver a proclamation, have a fireside chat over the radio, address the nation on television, tweet out policy decisions. There are so many words associated with the president. At their libraries, you can see volume after volume of written material related to their time in office, can turn every page if you're so inclined.

There's this story about Calvin Coolidge: he was the last true small-government Republican, the last one to hold a consistent policy of laissez-faire governing. What are we supposed to say about a man who said so little, whose reticence, almost a century later, is the thing most people know about him?

Do we tell the story of the Boston police strike and how his skills in negotiation as governor of Massachusetts put him on the road to joining the Republican ticket in 1920? Do we tell the story of how he tried to pass an anti-lynching bill at a time when the Klan was resurgent in the country, only to be blocked by Southern Democrats? Do we tell a story about how he won re-election after assuming the presidency, the first vice president to do so? Do we tell the story about how Ronald Reagan hung a portrait of Coolidge in the Oval Office?

Perhaps it is best for him if we stay silent. Quietly, we can look at him, or to him, or past him to what comes after—a stock market crash fueled by the lack of government oversight; a dedication to isolationism from Europe and Asia that we don't correct until it's too late; a wall of non-communication between the president and the people.

We may say that we love him, maybe claim his kinship, maybe hang a portrait of him. We can ask questions of him into the dark and see who doesn't answer. We've already said too much, broken a fragile silence with our clanging tongues. The damage was done. We lost.

Welcome Home, Mister President

Herbert Hoover
Thirty-first President of the United States
1929-1933
142 years since the Constitution
66 years since Emancipation
41 years until the resignation

Retirement: it little profits that an idle king, of course, but what else is he supposed to do in the thirty-two years after his sole term? When you are born in the Midwest, you leave the Midwest, only coming home to be buried there. He's not ready for West Branch yet.

Three decades and a year in the Waldorf Towers, an entire generation from leaving the White House to dying in Suite 31-A, and in all that time he sees only one other Republican president. His fault, really, or maybe the fault of being the wrong man at the wrong time. When the market crashed, what could he do? To arrest a thing like that would require a massive influx of . . . something. Federal money. Federal intervention. Shackling the free market. Best not to waste time speculating on what might have worked. He's an engineer. You can't put the water back behind the dam after the cracks widen and it floods the valley. Don't cross the water god.

He was the wunderkind, trusty Herbert, Stanford's best and brightest. Hadn't he fed Belgium during the first war? Hadn't he served ably as Secretary of Commerce, housing over a million people displaced in the 1927 Great Mississippi Flood? Hadn't he done well enough to win his first-ever campaign and become the president? He was the golden boy, the clever one. He could manage logistics and red tape, weaving together the threads of public and private enterprise to change the world.

He won the 1928 election in what we'd call a landslide, even peeling off some of the supposedly Solid South's electoral votes from the

Democrats. In his inaugural, he pledged to drive poverty even further from American life. Seven months later, the stock market crashed. The unemployment rate went from 3.2 percent to 8.7 percent between his first year and his second; by the third, the Dust Bowl had blanketed out the sky in the Plains, and the rate doubled again. When he left office, a quarter of the country's working force was idle. He'd lost the election—his second one, ever—by a greater margin than he'd won it four years earlier.

All his promise and hope of earlier days had unraveled. He left Washington and went not to Iowa, not to California, but to the Waldorf Astoria in New York City, a hotel whose name comes from the German ("forest settlement") and John Jacob Astor. A rich man's town in a single building.

In the lobby of the hotel—not the towers, those have their own private entrance off 50th Street—stands a clock, two tons in all, from 1893, when he was nineteen. The best presidents are on it, of course—Washington, Jackson, Lincoln— and Grant is there as the savior of the Union. Queen Victoria and Benjamin Franklin too. And then Grover Cleveland and Benjamin Harrison, simply by virtue of sharing their presidencies with that year. Two caretaker presidents welcoming home the president who watched the country crash. How galling. How insulting. No one sets out to be terrible at this job, not even mediocre. Caretakers. An insult in relief on the clock's faces: the greats, the forgettable, and then there's him, as though he fiddled as Wall Street took down the rest of the country, as though he was lashed to the mast and never did anything. For the best, really, that he never has to see the clock, that it's only for the hotel guests. He has that private entrance.

In this way passes retirement, some work of noble note. He writes books—one on fishing, one on mining, one on Wilson, more; he feeds the children of West Germany at Truman's request (Truman he can stand, unlike FDR, who took Hoover's name off that dam in Nevada). The Republicans bring him each year to their convention, the paraded pet, until 1964, when he's too ill to watch them shoot themselves by nominating Goldwater. What's the story about Odysseus's dog recognizing him after twenty years? Wasn't it by the smell? Didn't the dog die right afterward?

Suite 31-A. Home. A staff that knows him. A view out the window to midtown Manhattan. A long way from Iowa. These are his comforts, the pleasures of the idle king. In October of '64, just before LBJ demolishes Goldwater in the election, Herbert Hoover dies. They'll bring his body down from the suite—discreetly, of course; one imagines the service elevator—to a waiting car. Then home to West Branch, the holy city, a home that always waited for him, a home not to be renovated, turned into usable space, and rented out to the next tenant. His home at last, to rest finally, to rest forever, to retire for all time and drift no more, West Branch his Syracuse, Iowa his Ithaca, the unraveling finally set aside, next to the still hearth.

What the WPA Did in Carroll County, Iowa

Franklin D. Roosevelt
Thirty-second President of the United States
1933-1945
146 years since the Constitution
70 years since Emancipation
29 years until the resignation

They built the cemetery in the county seat, a granite gateway through which the dead and the living could pass. They cleared trees and brush. In Breda, in the northwest corner of the county, they constructed curbs and gutters for the town's streets. They did a sewing project, a surplus commodity survey, they built seventy miles of new roads for farmers to get their goods to market. In Coon Rapids, in the southeast corner, they built a storm-sewer system, which meant that when the storms came, the streets of Coon Rapids would no longer flood, which meant that the lives and livelihoods of its citizens, including May and George Duncan, Loretta and Floyd Rafferty, my paternal great-grandparents, were improved. The Administrated Works had effected Progress.

When I think of Franklin Roosevelt, the New Deal—that alphabet soup of agencies and organizations designed to lift the United States out of the Great Depression—is what comes to mind. I know he interned American citizens in our own concentration camps while the German camps ran full blast. I know he tried to pack the Supreme Court with extra judges who would favor his programs. I know he did things that could be considered tyrannical, but FDR is where the presidency becomes personal to me, because of the time that he put pen to paper and created an agency that came to rural Iowa and made improvements, and, perhaps more importantly, he gave those out of work a job and a purpose and the dignity that comes with that.

The WPA wrote reports: "Carroll County, in normal years, with adequate farm prices is generally able to take care of itself." Nineteen thirty-six is not a normal year, the nation still in the grip of depression, and in Carroll County, a drought and grasshopper invasion. I imagine it feels a little like the end of the world. Richard "Dick" Rafferty and Geraldine "Jerri" Duncan are teenagers. I don't know if they've met yet. Coon Rapids is a small town. The North Side bar and the South Side bar are on opposite sides of the same street. The two families likely know each other already.

Roosevelt was wealthy, from the kind of family that not only would have weathered the Depression but also profited somehow from it, and yet we might consider him a traitor to that world of privilege. When King George V visited the United States, the Roosevelts hosted him at Hyde Park and served hot dogs, acknowledging both the austerity necessary to perform during the Depression but also demonstrating a little bit of American pluck.

We were broke, we were struggling. In his second inaugural address, Roosevelt described the *millions whose daily lives in city and on farm continue under conditions labeled indecent by a so-called polite society half a century ago.* He had come from that polite society, and he chose to defy its structures and standards. Let them eat hot dogs.

The WPA gave people a job, hired when no one was hiring. On March 6, 1936, the WPA employed about thirty-seven thousand people in Iowa, two hundred and thirteen in Carroll County. By September 4, down to nineteen thousand and just eighty-three in Carroll County. The harvest had to come in, which meant the farms were hiring again.

By 1937, the crops had rebounded enough that Floyd Rafferty, who managed the Lyric Theater, could invest in air-conditioning and a remodeling. When his son Dick returned from the war almost a decade later, he worked there and would one day propose to Jerri while sweeping up after a show. He was a disabled veteran with a job. Work is a kind of dignity.

Even coming from America's polite society, Franklin Delano Roosevelt knew this. He'd known what it was like to have ambitions and suddenly find himself derailed by what happened to his body. He knew misfortune can happen to anyone, and that labor could be the solution. He'd taught himself to walk in braces despite the pain of it. He designed and built his own wheelchair. He understood that forced idleness is poison to the soul. He understood what having a purpose could mean.

The WPA sent the writers through the county. No painters to put a mural on the post office's walls, but the writers passed through and took note of what they saw: the Merle Hay Monument, Swan Lake State Preserve, the landscape, where "rolling hills appear like waves on the vast prairie, soft crumbling bluffs line the banks of rivers and streams." If you are traveling through Carroll County, you can still see these things. When I visited my grandmother, I could navigate automatically through the streets to the house on 7th Avenue where she lived since her marriage to my grandfather, the house to which my infant father returned from the hospital in the county seat, born nine months and one day after their marriage, driving down streets lined with storm drains installed eleven years earlier. When she died, I found my way to the Ohde Funeral Home along the same roads.

Roosevelt worked himself to death. Like Wilson's during the first World War, his brain hemorrhaged under the stress and strain of conducting the war. To see photos of him in 1945 is to see a man at the end of his capability. He is gaunt, dark circles under his eyes, his face lined deeply with care and concern and exhaustion. He was sixty-three and had served twelve years as president. He died at the beginning of his fourth term, a feat not only unmatched by any other president but also now impossible, thanks to the 22nd Amendment. We will literally never see another president like him.

I don't mean to suggest that my family owes its existence to Franklin Roosevelt. I don't know if it does or not. What FDR means to me, though, is an understanding of how the presidency can affect everyday people. I was born a generation and a half after he died, and yet he still seems real to me in a way that Hoover and all other preceding presidents do not. I feel—absurdly—like I know him, and all the presidents that follow, and that gives me license to judge them in a different way. One man in Washington signs a piece of paper, and a family in Iowa changes as a result, this time for the better. Perhaps that is why I shut my eyes to the darker parts of his presidency.

The WPA made maps and built roads, did what was necessary to get by, and their legacy was a generation that believed that the job of the federal government was to protect its citizens from the worst of capitalism, a government for the people. And they passed this belief down through their sons and daughters, grandsons and granddaughters. But I know, too, that FDR created an agency that gave ordinary people a reason to push on through the dark, an agency that hired a man to walk through the cemeteries of Carroll County and record the names, writing down Owen Rafferty and Edward and Effie Rafferty, all the Duncans and Pevestorfs and Herrons and Mahans, passing over the ground in which George and May and Floyd and Loretta and Dick and Jerri would all lie, writing down the names, all the names, a pen scratching each one down, because that was his job, and it was how he would live.

Infinity Room

Harry S Truman
Thirty-third President of the United States
1945-1953
158 years since the Constitution
82 years since Emancipation
21 years until the resignation

which is a room so contaminated with nuclear waste, byproducts of bomb-making, that it is sealed and can never be opened again; a room that to step inside it without safety gear means certain death; a room in which ordinary things—gloves, a hammer, a chair—have become Death, the destroyer of worlds; a room that will always exist but did not exist until the day Harry Truman, newly president, Roosevelt's brain having bled out thirteen days earlier, first steps into the infinity room,

which is a room in the White House in which Henry Stimson, the Secretary of War, looks the new president in the face—a new president after twelve steady years of Roosevelt, after four and a half years of the world at war, after three and a half years of America at war, with the knowledge of Nanking, Bataan, Iwo Jima, Okinawa, with the Soviets (26 million dead) at the gates of Berlin and plans made for the American invasion of Japan (possibly a million American casualties, they assume, twice the number of dead so far)—he looks him in the face and says *Sir, there is a weapon*, and Truman closes his eyes and finds himself in the infinity room,

which is a field in France in 1918, where young Lieutenant Truman directs artillery fire onto a different German army. He is seeing the physical toll of war: the scarred faces, the mangled horses, the ground itself torn open by the shells he fires to kill other men. He breathes air free for now of phosgene or mustard gas, knows their telltale scents (new-mown hay, garlic), knows poison, knows bombs, knows what a dying soldier in an invaded country looks and sounds like as he takes his last breath, for he has seen them in the infinity room,

which is a doctor's office in Independence, Missouri, in which a young boy is fitted for his first pair of eyeglasses. He is no longer short-sighted, no longer far-sighted; for the first time, he can see clearly what is before him: the doctor, the lamp, the chart on the wall, the door that leads to the infinity room,

which is on the third floor of an office building in Hiroshima;

which is in the basement of a house in Nagasaki;

which is on an island in Pennsylvania; a farmer's field in Ukraine; a ranch in New Mexico; each one leads us to a new place, the infinity room,

which is an old man's bedroom in Independence, which has always been here. His glasses are on the nightstand. Some people ask him how he can live with the bombs' weight, how the shadows burned into the walls of the cities do not haunt him at every moment. He tells them that he *never lost any sleep*, the buck stopping bluntly with him before leading once more into the infinity room,

which is a military warehouse that is storing half a million Purple Hearts, medals ordered in advance of an invasion that never happened. Enough medals to carry us through the dead and wounded of Korea, of Vietnam, of Iraq and Afghanistan and dozens of other incursions and intrusions around the world, with a hundred thousand or so still remaining in their dark boxes, waiting for their presentation to the survivors, while the doors of the infinity room open again and again and again, revealing to us the impossible choices we ask mortals to make.

Kansas, She Said, Is the Name of the Stat

Dwight D. Eisenhower
Thirty-fourth President of the United States
1953-1961
166 years since the Constitution
90 years since Emancipation
13 years until the resignation

Eisenhower as Farmhands

He's whatever we need him to be, plays whatever role we need him to fill. Before he is able to give the orders, he must follow them. After the war, both parties court him as a candidate. At the end, Dorothy looks at the farmhands from her bed: "And you, and you, and you . . . were there." They laugh, and she concludes, "But you couldn't have been, could you?"

Eisenhower as Auntie Em and Uncle Henry

There's no place like home but this, a two-story frame house in Denison, Texas, just over the border from Oklahoma. He is born there, and then his family returns to Kansas eighteen months later. He'll have no memory of this home, although he'll return after the war, and again as candidate, and again as former president. Remember: home is a place to which we are always trying to return.

Eisenhower as Professor Marvel

He's an old Kansas man himself, born and bred in the heart of the western wilderness. Where he grows up, he is as far from saltwater as he can be, an ocean of wheat on either side of him.

Eisenhower as Dorothy

A great war comes. He is a young man, transported from Kansas. To reach the war, the army mobilizes over terrible roads. At night, his bones rattled from potholes and washboards, he dreams of a gleaming

108

system of roads rising above the country, crossing it, linking its cities, a road to follow wherever it might go.

Eisenhower as Tin Man

Another war on the same continent. This time he is in charge, Supreme Allied Commander. When he sends the men to the beaches to fight and die and perhaps succeed, what does he feel? A sorrow? A hope? A heartbreaking? In his headquarters, he waits for the news to arrive, his heart beating faster and faster.

Eisenhower as Scarecrow

He watches over the barbed-wire field, the birds frightened away by his approach. The living here are more scarecrow than he, but they are fallen, empty husks of men. The crows might return to the camp, so he watches, witnesses.

Eisenhower as Wizard

After the war, he drifts for a while—NATO chief, memoirist, university president— before he enters politics and then the White House. Professor Marvel: "Suddenly, the wind changed direction and the balloon floated down into the heart of this noble city, where I was instantly acclaimed Oz, the First Wizard Deluxe. Times being what they were, I accepted the job." He uses smoke and mirrors to speak to the press and nation. He builds his road. They ask him questions: *Russia? East Germany? A place called Indochina?* He has learned how to answer without answering. Pay no attention to the man behind the curtain.

Eisenhower as Cowardly Lion

A new look: NSC 162/2. A report. Build more of those weapons, he says. Enough to destroy the enemy a dozen, a hundred times over. He remembers waiting for the reports from Normandy. He remembers the relief of not invading Japan, the million American lives exchanged for a quarter million of theirs. The bomb is a good. He is not afraid.

Eisenhower as Wicked Witch of the West

"You have a row of dominos set up, you knock over the first one, and what will happen to the last one is a certainty that it will go over very quickly."

Eisenhower as Toto

At the end, he understands. In his farewell address, he warns of the military-industrial complex, shows its machinations at work, trying to pull back the curtain. What can one small dog nipping at the heels of giants do? Even he, once a titan, is worn down by eight years. He sees Vietnam. He is predicting here, a map of Iraq, Afghanistan, more for us to discover behind the curtain.

Eisenhower as Glinda

He retires to the battlefield, quiet now, a Gettysburg farmhouse. There's no place that's home but this. When he dies, years later, they put his body in a simple soldier's casket and send it back to Kansas, to Abilene, from which the interstate highway runs, white dashes dividing the lanes, blurring together into a single line as they pick up speed, trying their best to follow it home.

I Ask My Father, Sixteen in Sixty-Three, Where He Was When He Heard the News

John F. Kennedy
Thirty-fifth President of the United States
1961-1963
158 years since the Constitution
98 years since Emancipation
11 years until the resignation

I. For the last few seconds of his life, he's in pain, from at least Frame 225, when he re-emerges from behind the sign blocking Zapruder's view, to Frame 313, when his life ends, about three and a half seconds. In the film, he is reacting, his hands rising to the wound in his throat. How quickly does shock set in? How much trauma before a body stops understanding pain? Could it happen in those few seconds?

II. My father tells me: "I was in seventh-period study hall, and this teacher came in and said 'there's a news bulletin that the president's been shot and killed.' And he was, he was a jerk, this teacher, and he said it in this flip way, not happy, but flip. They didn't cancel school. We just went home at the end of the day. I don't really remember my parents reacting to it a whole lot. I didn't think at that time *I can't believe the president's dead*, but more like *What just happened? What's going on?*

"I do remember that night I had to go to Carroll with my friend John Lloyd so he could buy a blue suit, I don't remember why he needed a suit, what does a sixteen-year-old boy need a blue suit for? We drove to Carroll, the county seat, ten thousand people, where there was a bunch of nice clothing stores. It was Friday night, and this was 1963, of course, so people still did their shopping downtown, the shops were open late, until nine, and the sidewalks were just packed with people, and I remember seeing newsboys on the street—actual newsboys holding papers: *Extra! extra! read all about it!* I'd never seen that before.

111

"And, you know, it didn't really sink in until that night. Grandpa Duncan had just had a heart attack, so there were all these relatives in and out of the house. The TV was on all the time those days—we watched the funeral, my uncle Bill and I watched Ruby shoot Oswald live, and we were like 'What the hell just happened?' By then, we felt this sadness, this loss.

"But the nonstop news. And the newsboys in Carroll. That's what I remember."

He pauses, stops. There's a caesura, a pause, a break here. What else is there to say?

III. "Words alone are not enough," Kennedy would have said that Friday afternoon at the Municipal Auditorium.

IV. We lack words for pain, defaulting instead to numbers on a scale or a cartoon face that suggests how we feel.

Kennedy spent his life in pain, agonizing with very little relief on most of his days. Even before the football injury that hurt his back, he'd suffered from illness throughout his childhood. The family joke was that any mosquito that bit him would soon die.

Everything he did hurt: the five-hour swim after PT-109 sank, which he did towing an injured crewman via a lifejacket strap clenched in his teeth; the campaigns for the House and the Senate and the White House; the standoff against Cuba and the Soviet Union; the phone calls to southern governors, trying to negotiate equality; the speeches that inspired a generation. Look at the smiles he flashes at the cameras or the careful gestures he makes during a speech, and see if you can see the pain behind them.

He received last rites at least three times before the last time in Dallas. Surgeons operated on his back four times, attempting to ease his pain by screwing a plate to the base of his spine. One operation left a hole that became infected, leaking pus and blood and even bits of bone. He never said a word about it, said one of his aides.

He met Khrushchev in Vienna and negotiated poorly, possibly because of the pain, possibly because of the methamphetamine shots his doctor administered beforehand. He was wearing his back brace in Dallas, which meant that he did not slump into the seat after the first shot, the one he might have survived. Instead he stayed somewhat upright, the back of his head facing the book depository. How much did his pain change history? Is Kennedy the open wound of America? The unanswered question? The perpetual *what if?* of our country. He would have realized the folly of Vietnam and pulled us out before too long, we say. He would have saved us from the downward slide into riots and rebellions and revolutions, political and cultural and otherwise, we say. He would have done so much, if only, if only.

Nostalgia, a word born from the Greek *algos,* meaning *pain.* Kennedy creates that caesura of suffering, the unspoken answer, the end of possibilities. My father can tell the story of where he was, just like anyone of his generation, but there will always be the pause at the end. Words alone are not enough.

Cato/Caro

Lyndon B. Johnson
Thirty-Sixth President of the United States
1963-1969
176 years since the Constitution
100 years since Emancipation
5 years to the resignation

This must be love; why else explore the labyrinth, unwinding his thread behind him, for so long? Why chase a man he can never meet, to write his story? Why begin by announcing his intentions for a trilogy, and as the years pass, find it growing, moving beyond its original borders, until he finds himself toeing the edge of the jungle (literally—he entered the metaphorical jungle decades ago) to understand the war his subject neither began nor ended but for which he is known, the chanting in front of the White House first and nationwide later (*Hey, hey / LBJ / how many kids /did you kill today?*) to write the fifth— fifth!—book of this trilogy?

The average age of those boys who went to the jungle was just nineteen, and here he is, ten years past his allotted threescore and ten, on the edge of the summit. He has won all the awards that matter, published over three thousand pages on him, and only now has reached the meat of this presidency. He is Robert Caro, biographer of Lyndon Baines Johnson. Caro never met Johnson, but he has devoted his life to him.

In the spring of 1778, while camped at Valley Forge, General George Washington, violating a ban on theatrical performances, organized a performance of Joseph Addison's 1713 tragedy *Cato* for his men. The play's themes—noble sacrifice in support of republican virtues and in resistance to tyranny—would, one hopes, have energized the tired Continental soldiers, still three years from Yorktown's final victory.

114

And Washington, watching the play's end, in which the Roman senator Cato falls upon his sword rather than be captured by the dictator Caesar's advancing army—Washington, whose father and two brothers died ahead of their threescore and ten—what did he think of the play he had arranged? Watching that ending (*Let us bear this awful corpse to Caesar, / and lay it in his sight, that it may stand / a fence betwixt us and the victor's wrath*), did he think about losing the war? Did he think about the hangman's noose, reserved for traitors? Did he see himself as a fence between the crown and his boys?

Boys, I need you, Johnson calls over the ranch house intercom. *Send Mike immediately*. When the Secret Service arrives, they find him already dead. The Paris Peace Accords, ending U.S. military involvement in Vietnam, are signed five days later.

Let us bear this awful corpse to Caesar.

Washington rides his horse in a snowstorm, eats dinner in wet clothes, and dies two days later. Washington warned against alliances with foreign nations in his farewell address, although *we may safely trust to temporary alliances for extraordinary emergencies*. The Gulf of Tonkin was the point of the labyrinth where we realized how far from the entrance we were, perhaps where we looked back for Ariadne's thread and could not find it.

Extraordinary emergency. Norman Morrison, a year later, sets himself on fire outside of the Secretary of Defense's window at the Pentagon. The thing to ask is not what a man must believe to set himself on fire, but what makes him decide at the moment before he poured the kerosene on himself and struck the match to drop his infant daughter. The thing to wonder about is how the daughter might not have been afraid until the moment her father let her go so that he could become the awful corpse, flames ten feet high, according to witnesses.

This is the fear: that the work will never be finished. Chase the ghosts from the Texas Hill Country to the jungle of Vietnam, but the fear is that the truth can never be complete. Caro in an introduction discusses two threads of Johnson's life—the bright one that did its damnedest to create a Great Society, passing civil rights legislation, Medicare and education bills, even highway beautification programs, and the dark one that stole a Congressional election, that bullied senators and everyone else, that ignored intelligence and advisers and steadily escalated the war in Vietnam.

This fear of never finishing—that's Addison's Cato, *severely bent against himself / renouncing sleep, and rest, and food, and ease.* That's Lincoln, in his second inaugural address, *Let us strive on to finish the work we are in.* That's Caro, working on the fifth volume in his eightieth year, a volume covering the country's division. That's any biographer, split between the blank page and the blinking cursor and the stack of research. That's America, now fractured against itself, always on the verge of burning, or breaking, or breaking through.

Our lives, discolored with our present woes / may still grow bright, and smile with happier hours.

The thing to keep thinking about is LBJ in 1928 in the South Texas town of Cotulla, teaching at the "Mexican school," buying equipment with his own salary. This seems so human, in ways that might be the opposite of Kennedy, who never watched anyone, much less children, dig through garbage piles to find grapefruit rinds with a little bit of pulp left. A man doesn't forget a thing like that.

Or is that the fault of the biographer's impulse? They fall in love, and they don't want to lift the dark thread. They follow the bright thread because it takes them where they want to go, out of the labyrinth. It's good to think about Washington turning down a lifetime of power twice. It's less good to think about him owning other humans, less good to think about him in the nascent nation's capital of Philadelphia, sending his cook Hercules back to Virginia to avoid the Pennsylvania laws that freed any slave who had been in the state for six months. It's good to think about LBJ saying *We shall overcome.* It's good to think about LBJ inviting Martin Luther King, Jr. to the White House for the signing of the Civil Rights Act. Follow the thread that can never run out, until it does, and then look at what's at the center of the labyrinth: the person you love, or the Minotaur. Or can he be both? Can his final acts on this earth be to entrust his child to a stranger, and then to burn?

Else whence this pleasing hope, this fond desire / this longing after immortality?

What the best biographers hold close is a mature love, even if they dare not call it that. Not the child's love of the parent, in which the good is amplified and the bad ignored (or worse, justified), but the love of the adult, embracing the mistakes and flaws, the full acknowledgment of the person loved. Devotion without erasure. Washington, Lincoln, Cato, Caro, all of them—ambition pressed into the service of something greater than them: nation, art, whatever. The best of what we might become despite—or even in part because of—the dark thread.

Or whence this secret dread, and inward horror / of falling into nought?

Caro will finish the work he is in, and will show us a few years of an America that constantly evolves, not in a linear way but in an evolutionary way: false starts, dead ends, reversals, but eventually, slowly forward. The American paradox: how to be *more* perfect? The resolution: fits and starts. A maze.

Through what new scenes and changes must we pass! / The wide, th' unbounded prospect, lies before me; / but shadows, clouds and darkness, rest upon it. / Here will I hold.

Boys and girls, America needs you.

[expletive deleted]

Richard Nixon
Thirty-seventh President of the United States
1969-1974
182 years since the Constitution
103 years since Emancipation
Resigned the office in 1974

1.   For a year and seven months, after Truman dies in December 1972 and LBJ follows in January 1973, but before Gerald Ford assumes the office in August 1974, Richard Nixon is the only living president. He is the only person who knows what the awesome power and responsibilities of the office entail, the only person who knows what it's like to hold the highest office in the land. In those nineteen months, there are twelve men who know what it's like to walk on the moon and one man who knows what it's like to sit in the Oval Office as Commander-in-Chief.

2.   Here is a man already prone to feeling left out—who had started his own club, the Orthogonians, at Whittier College when the Franklins, the established club, would not let him join—who is now more isolated than at any time previous. Here is a man whose downfall comes at his own hands, at his insistence on recording every conversation, every rant, every private discussion of matters big and small in his office.

3.   Perhaps, as much as he is a man defined by recordings, he is a man defined by gaps. The constant [expletive deleted] in the tape transcripts. The eighteen-and-a-half minute gap in the Watergate tapes that is supposedly an accidental erasure by his secretary, stretched out to answer the phone, and whose contents have puzzled historians for two generations. The gap of his unfinished presidency, filled by Ford, a man who became president by virtue of Nixon's choice.

4.   I was born in the bicentennial year, in the wake of the resignation. During my entire childhood, no president died, and then, the month I graduated from high school, Nixon died. I remember the platitudes, the praise for his foreign policy triumphs. In the papers, the photo of him on Air Force One in China, arriving to meet with Mao. He was the president to begin the removal of American troops from Vietnam.

5.   Some remember him that way. Some remember him as the disgraced former president, the only one to resign the office, who conducted secret wars and who more than likely approved dirty tricks to secure his re-election. They remember that before he removed the troops from Vietnam, securing a "peace with honor," his signature was on several thousand condolence letters to families across the country.

6.   How does presidents get remembered? How do they move into our national memory? How does the memory get set, if it ever does? How do we isolate them into the story that we tell? That becomes the history by which we understand ourselves? If there's no one else who knows what it's like to bear the weight of the job, then how did Nixon understand the presidency? How could we understand it?

7.   He had it written on his own tombstone: "The greatest honor History can bestow is the title of Peacemaker," which he had said in his first inaugural address.

8.   That eighteen-and-a-half minute gap, the one that Rose Mary Woods said she'd caused accidentally while stretching to answer the phone—no one knows what was on it. The gap is in the middle of a conversation between Nixon and his Chief of Staff, H. R. Haldeman. Nixon said he didn't remember what they'd discussed. Haldeman's notes mentioned that they discussed the break-in at the Watergate Complex.

9.   Does that history matter? The tapes from three days later weren't erased, and their contents, once made public, were enough to make the remaining support for Nixon vanish. He resigned a few days later.

10.   Haldeman's successor, Alexander Haig, said that "a sinister force" was responsible for the erasure. Maybe history is the sinister force, erasing Nixon to either foreign policy genius or disgraced, resigned president.

11.   There are so many ways that the story of Richard Nixon should be a shining example of the American spirit. His father ran a gas station and grocery store in Yorba Linda, California, the opposite of the tony upbringing of Kennedy. Nixon wanted to play football in both high school and college despite his small stature, and did, technically, as a rarely used substitute more known for his cheering than his playing time. He left California for Duke Law School, all the way across the country, and rose to be elected president of its bar association, graduating third in his class. He served in the navy in World War II, and then started his political career with a series of wins—first a representative, then a senator, then Ike's vice president, before he lost the presidency to Kennedy by a thin margin in 1960, and then lost the California governor's race in 1962.

12.   Those are stories history tells us: the debates on television and his five o'clock shadow dooming him while the golden Kennedy shines; him stating *You won't have Nixon to kick around anymore* to the press after the loss in '62.

13.   It would be easy to count him out then, but he returns in 1968 and wins, and then buries McGovern in a landslide in 1972. This is the kind of story we love in America—the idea that anyone, even a grocer's son from small-town California, can become president, can face the odds again and again, can make sacrifices, can stand up to his defeats to come back swinging and win.

14. 　　Deep Throat told the journalists the White House tapes had been manipulated. He was standing in a parking garage in northern Virginia that was supposed to be torn down, erased from the landscape in 2017, and yet still stands, mute witness.

15. 　　Which Nixon do we walk into history with? Depends on who's telling the story, and to whom, and when. It is possible that we're so close to this history that we can't hold onto all of it. When I think of LBJ, I think of a man in black-and-white, and when I think of Nixon, I think of a man in color.

16. 　　The first time I left the country, I went to Beijing. I was able to visit China in large part because Nixon had gone to China before I was born and changed the relationship between two countries in ways that have rippled far out into today and will continue into tomorrow. Our tour guide took us to one of the approved restaurants for tourists to get Peking duck, and on the wall was a photograph of Nixon in that restaurant—not him in the triumph of 1972 but during his return visit in retirement in 1985. He was an old man in that photo. Old in a way that I never thought of him.

17. 　　How will we remember today in fifty years? As a sinister force? As a triumph of foreign policy?

18. 　　Nixon's tombstone is black granite. It says that the greatest title history can bestow is "peacemaker," but it leaves it to us to determine if Nixon received that title.

18.5. 　　(note to self: redact the unimportant parts?)

Gaffe

Gerald Ford
Thirty-eighth President of the United States
1974-1977
187 years since the Constitution
111 years since Emancipation
Immediately following the resignation

Find the camera with the red light. That's the live one. Look into it. The lights they've brought to the Palace of Fine Arts will blind you, make it impossible to see much beyond the perimeter, beyond the moderator, beyond the panelists, beyond your opponent.

There's an audience out there. More watching at home. You've agreed to these debates, a chance to show that you, Gerald Ford, are your own man. No one elected you, after all, to anything since your seat in Congress. There was the whirlwind: the bribes, the break-in, the hearings, the helicopter on the White House lawn—and then you were here.

You've got something to prove. Consider the struggle ahead of you: for generations, the American people believed they could trust the federal government, that it was on the side of the good guys, the ones who didn't start a war without cause, who fought for noble causes, who believed in fair play and following the rules. Something broke in the last few years, shattering when the Plumbers got up to their dirty tricks in the Watergate, but also when Daniel Ellsberg leaked the Pentagon Papers and showed that the government knew the conflict in Vietnam was a lost cause long before they stopped feeding men into the maw of that war. Something broke in us then. Now it's your job to rally the team and lead us to victory.

They've made you up before airtime, trying to turn you into a better version of yourself. You know the story about Dick and his terrible makeup in '60, about the five o'clock shadow and the sweat. People who listened on the radio thought he'd won. People who watched on TV said Jack did. And then Jack won.

Dick's in Yorba Linda now, retired. He didn't do this television nonsense again anyway—fool me once, etc, etc. Improper for the incumbent.

But you've got something to prove. You need to win. Not just for the office, but for you. Legitimacy. Honor. All that sort of thing. *Victory with honor,* ha-ha.

So the makeup: powder to start, to take the shine away. The face produces oil, the oil makes you look sweaty, sweat makes you look like a failure. You are not a failure. You played football, at Michigan too, and you actually played, not like Dick riding the pine at his Quaker college. You turned down the Lions and the Packers to coach at Yale while you studied the law.

They use a foam rubber sponge, a wedge, to apply a layer, maybe two, of foundation to your face, ears, neck. They tuck tissues into your collar to keep it from staining. It's all supposed to look natural. In another room, someone else is working on your opponent's face in the same way, evening him out, smoothing his edges.

He doesn't know what this is like. Even in your less-than-a-term first term, you've had two people try to kill you, one in this very city. Inflation, recession, a pardon for Dick. Saigon falling. Kissinger, for God's sake. The press. That comedian on the live show, the new one, in New York, who imitates you via pratfalls and mishaps, despite the fact that you have always demonstrated such mastery over how the body moves.

That comedian looks nothing like you.

Look in the Palace's mirror: you look like you. A better you. All the problem areas smoothed away, hidden under the makeup. They've even brushed your eyebrows.

Now you're on stage. Find that red light. The sound works this time, thank God. At the first debate, it went out, and while they fixed it, you both stood there, frozen, neither of you willing to relax, to let down your guard. You're always presenting your best self, your impossible self. You were planning on retiring when Dick came to you with his request.

After Kennedy's assassination in Dallas, they turned to you and six others to figure it out. You did. Your name's on the front of that report. You know the damage a few seconds can do. You know about a magic bullet. You know how a season's worth of statistics can be lost in a single fumble. You've got a record of 13-0 in your elections.

So be careful. You're live. Give them nothing to point at and say, "Aha! We told you he was an accident. We told you he was flawed."

The second debate is foreign policy. Your opponent, behind in the polls, comes at you like a boxer. "He's weak," he says. Says you don't know how to do it. Says Kissinger's the president when it comes to matters like this.

The panelist from the *New York Times* asks you about the Soviet Union's hand in Eastern Europe. Time for toughness. Leadership. Fourth and goal. You'll show them who a real president is. You say: *There is no Soviet domination of Eastern Europe, and there never will be under a Ford administration.*

Oh, no. Did you just say that? Do you know what you just said? Workers' strikes in Poland this summer, the news suppressed by the authorities. A sham election in Romania last year, where no candidate could run without the Party's approval. Even the *New York Times* man can't believe what you just said.

"I'm sorry . . . did I understand you to say, sir, that the Soviets are not using Eastern Europe as their own sphere of influence in occupying most of the countries there?"

Game time. No flaws. Best self. If the sound goes out, don't move. If you give an answer, stand by it. The bullet will turn in midair. Time to make the highlight reel. You say: *I don't believe that the Yugoslavians consider themselves dominated by the Soviet Union. I don't believe that the Romanians consider themselves dominated by the Soviet Union. I don't believe that the Poles consider themselves dominated by the Soviet Union. Each of these countries is independent, autonomous, it has its own territorial integrity, and the United States does not concede that those countries are under the domination of the Soviet Union.*

Best self. Strong leader. President of all of it, especially on foreign policy. A statement like that defies whatever they might claim. You know this from personal experience, from having gone to Poland, Romania, and Yugoslavia, having spoken with citizens there, reassuring them that the United States president and its citizens stand with them in their resistance.

But you come up short. Your statement, boldly delivered, comes off as a gaffe, not a firm stance. And that's it. The clock has run out. When the red light turns off, wait for the all-clear. They'll use a remover to take off the foundation, to remove the powder, to strip you down. It's back to ordinary. Back to the flawed, blemished self. Every athlete has a moment when they know that is over. Do you have that now? Do you get the sense that this is where the decline begins, where the game began to slip away from you?

The few seconds after the request for clarification and before you answer—those will become your *What if.* Your *If only.* Your what might have happened. In a perfect world, you catch yourself, stop the fall, arrest the body's tyranny.

You had something to prove. You proved it's not a perfect world. You proved that a man can take the field with every intention of dominating his opponent and suddenly find himself outmatched. You proved that a single mistake can undo everything, can be the way that they define you for the rest of your life.

Pardon

Jimmy Carter
Thirty-ninth President of the United States
1977-1981
190 years since the Constitution
114 years since Emancipation
3 years since the resignation

All have sinned and fallen short of the glory of God.

A country built on stolen land and by stolen labor, through revolution and annexation, the hoodwinking of governments and the overthrowing of sovereign monarchies, and still we have the gall to say that our president may forgive the transgressions of citizens. These presidents, fallible men, flawed men, men who cut backroom deals, who slandered each other, who were unfaithful to their wives and their country, who are they to bestow a pardon upon the criminals of the United States?

We are a nation without the divine right of royalty, which made us dangerous in infancy, chaotic in adolescence, brutal in adulthood. Original sin? We ate the apples of knowledge across this land, finding them in Plymouth, in Lexington and Concord, in the slave markets of Charleston and Richmond and New York City, at the prison camps of Andersonville and Manzanar, at Iolani Palace and Fort Robinson. The president is as fallible as any of us—worse, maybe, if he thirsts for power. *All have sinned and fallen short of the glory of God.*

But he—a peanut farmer, Jefferson's dream—he may be different. In his Georgia county, he was the only white man who did not join the Concerned Citizens' Council, façade of the segregationists. He is *the voice of one crying in the wilderness* to lead us forward. We welcome him, accept him, a chance for restoration after we have fallen so far, from the balconies of the Watergate complex to the banks of the Potomac below. We look at the brokenness of America and we look to him to fix us together, to welcome us back to the fold.

126

When he takes the oath of office, he does so on a Bible his mother gave him, opened to Micah 6:8: *"What does the Lord require of thee, but to do justly, and to love mercy, and to walk humbly with thy God."*

He asks us if a country founded on liberty and spirituality can become what it once promised it would be. He asks if America can be a country that governs by a moral compass when it makes its decisions. Who believes that this is possible? Any inauguration, and his especially, is always a time for hope against our natures. Can we accomplish this goal?

He tries. He brings Egypt and Israel together at Camp David. He returns Panama its own canal. He sets what will become the United States Holocaust Memorial Museum into motion. He negotiates with his Soviet counterpart on limiting nuclear arms, signs a treaty.

On his first day in office, he signs a blanket pardon for the men who fled America rather than fight in Vietnam. His predecessor had offered a conditional pardon, but Jimmy Carter knows that love and forgiveness must be offered freely.

This is not a small group of prodigal sons. This is perhaps a half million men or more he calls home, for whom he has *killed the fattened calf.* These brothers of ours *were dead and are alive again, lost and are now found.*

He tries. What can he do? *Shall not the judge of all the earth do what is just?* He holds the codes to launch the fire that would scour the planet, and he wants to do good. Impossible. How quickly are promises of the campaign and good intentions of the first one hundred days pushed aside? This job murders men, this job murders men's souls. What does it profit the electorate to gain their souls but face stagflation at home and an aggressive Red Army moving abroad in Afghanistan and Cuba and who knows where else?

We shall not kill. We shall not bear false witness. We shall not covet our neighbor's goods. And yet the contradiction of this country includes all these things and more. We constantly move backward as we try to move forward. Perhaps we love this country because we are naïve, or because we keep envisioning what it might be, what it actually is in moments of glory and transfiguration, and so we might beg your pardon: pardon for believing that Jefferson, a slaveholder, could write *All men are created equal*; pardon for Lincoln, who signed both the Emancipation Proclamation and the execution order for thirty-nine Santee Sioux with the same hand; pardon for Truman, who bombed Hiroshima and integrated the armed forces; even pardon for Nixon, who ordered the break-in at the Watergate complex, sending us into a long spiral from which we have yet to recover. Pardon all of them. We all know what it is like to want to leave. We all know what it is like to want to come home. Of course, Carter served only a single term; he tried to make us consider the whole world, and our hearts—oh, our hearts, the ones that love power and money too much, that lust for what we do not have too often, that build walls around ourselves to block out the chances for breakthroughs and growing, frightened of what we might become in those vulnerable moments of shared humanity—our hearts are *wicked and deceitful* above all.

Dissolve To

Ronald Reagan
Fortieth President of the United States
1981-1989
194 years since the Constitution
118 years since Emancipation
7 years since the resignation

FADE IN—*An empty stage, dark except for a spotlight on a single stool. In the distance, we hear evidence of a crowd: murmuring, brief snatches of music, muted applause. Some sort of gathering is taking place, but what exactly, this is hidden from us.*

Into the frame walks the AUTHOR, tall, middle-aged white guy, glasses. He looks younger than he is, but he feels old. He sits on the stool.

AUTHOR: My memory switched on at the very end of the 1970s, but only for the big stuff—my little sister's birth, to be exact. I remember walking through snow with my father to the back of the hospital, and him lifting me up to the window to see my mother and sister.

It's a while before I'm aware of the world around me, bigger than my family and friends, bigger than the clearing we play in and the short street that is my universe. But when I am aware of that world, there he is, on the television and the newspaper, the one in charge, the first man I know as president.

Lights go up on REAGAN, standing stage left at a podium with the presidential seal, in a brown suit. Crowd noises get louder for a moment.

AUTHOR: I don't know why, but something unnerves me from the start. Maybe it's my parents' reaction to him. Maybe it's the perfect hair, the jar of jellybeans. Maybe it's the way he's always everywhere. I go to a Catholic school, where I learn about the omnipresence of God. Maybe it's that.

ENTER DUKE—yeah, him. *He's wearing nautical gear—a sou'wester hat and an oilskin coat. Good sideburns on him. He stands under a third spotlight. Crowd noises get louder than we've heard them before. He looks brave.*

DUKE: You startin' to tell my future?

AUTHOR: (*Looks back*) Only the end. (*To audience*) He, on the other hand, died earlier in 1979, before I can remember anything, but he's always there too. He reminds my mother of her father, who will die the next year. I've got a handful of memories of him, nothing much.

DUKE: Stop yawing and finish off! (*His light fades*)

AUTHOR: Anyway. There you are. Here's your ground situation: a young boy, the hard men, both actors, both performers. You can't break character if you're always playing yourself.

Lights up on DUKE again, who is now in a deep-sea diving suit.

DUKE: Bolt the faceplate on! (*One is bolted on. Two rubbery tentacles, ostensibly belonging to a prop giant squid, reach in, pulling him off stage. Both AUTHOR and REAGAN watch, then turn back. No crowd noise.*)

REAGAN: We are faced with the most evil enemy mankind has known in his long climb from the swamp to the stars.

AUTHOR: I understood story, and conflict, and character. I understood that there were good guys and bad guys. The lines seemed clearly drawn, the ending of the script already written. We would take this as far as it needed to go.

DUKE re-enters, this time in the uniform of a navy man—a Seabee, a member of the Construction Brigade.

DUKE: Sure, I've changed. I was never one for sitting on fences.

REAGAN: Well, one of the worst mistakes anybody can make is to bet against Americans.

AUTHOR: With us or against us, right? No middle ground. I was a ten-year-old who thought about nuclear weapons all the time.

I couldn't forget. There was nowhere to hide from it. Once I'd seen the old test footage—the black and white film in the Nevada desert, the side of the house bursting into flames before disintegrating—I couldn't forget it.

DUKE: Why didn't you stay in the bomb shelter?

REAGAN: The United States does not start fights. We will never be an aggressor. We maintain our strength in order to deter and defend against aggression—to preserve freedom and peace.

DUKE: Hold your fire 'til you get 'em under your guns—then let 'em have it! (*From offstage, a sniper's bullet hits DUKE. The wound is strangely bloodless. Lights down on him. Still no crowd noise.*)

AUTHOR: I was a ten-year-old boy who knew what Mutually Assured Destruction meant.

REAGAN: My fellow Americans, I am pleased to tell you I just signed legislation which outlaws Russia forever. The bombing begins in five minutes.

AUTHOR: He actually said that. I'm not making any of this up. They were testing a mic. I'd call it a gaffe if he hadn't built an entire career in front of microphones.

Lights up on DUKE, again, although he is now in a sea captain's hat and coat.

DUKE: Anyone else who wants to start a fight aboard this ship can see what he looks like when he's through.

REAGAN: There you go again. (*Crowd cheers*)

AUTHOR: It's a sore spot. Put him on the dime? Put him on Mount Rushmore? They laud him endlessly, sing his praises, hold him up as the purest of Republicans, but it's like they've never even considered him and what he actually did.

DUKE: You seem to know what you want, and I think I know what it is. (*He exits*)

AUTHOR: I want the roles to stop. I want an honest answer. I want a childhood where I didn't think about a mushroom cloud appearing over my school, where I didn't think about radiation poisoning. Are all children in all generations terrified of the things they can't control? Just mine? Just me? (*A few boos from the crowd*)

REAGAN: No weapon in the arsenals of the world is so formidable as the will and moral courage of free men and women.

DUKE re-enters, again in the deep-sea diving outfit.

AUTHOR: Says the guy who wanted lasers in space to shoot down missiles. (*Beat*) But, you know, I don't know. It's not like we had a nuclear war. Communism fell. I was scared of the bomb, but I also romanticized it. I admired Oppenheimer's determination. My family made a side trip to Los Alamos during vacation, my request. I remember—

DUKE: Here we are again, right back where we started. You got what you wanted—now I'm gonna get what I want. Alright, Jack! (*Faceplate on. From upstage, his air hose is severed. He pulls it to him, looks at it in horror, collapses. Lights down on him.*)

AUTHOR: He could bounce back. Nothing stuck. Remember, they called him the Teflon President. He even broke the Curse of Tecumseh, which had killed seven other presidents.

DUKE re-enters in military fatigues.

DUKE: I feel a lot better. Never felt so good in my life! How 'bout a cigarette? (*Again, DUKE is felled by a sniper's bullet. Lights down on him.*)

AUTHOR: Reagan, he gets shot, and in the emergency room, he's able to look at the surgeons and say—

REAGAN: I hope you're all Republicans. (*Crowd laughs*)

AUTHOR: And when his wife finally sees him, he can look at her and say—

REAGAN: Honey, I forgot to duck. (*Crowd laughs louder*)

AUTHOR: That's stage presence. That's impressive, maybe even admirable.

ENTER DUKE, this time in buckskin jacket and coonskin cap. He looks, for the first time, older.

DUKE: Another thing I promised Mother—never to get into situations where people pointed guns at me.

AUTHOR: You know neither of them fought in World War II? Reagan's eyesight kept him home, where he made training films with the 1st Motion Picture Unit. Wayne was deferred, 3-A, because of his family, and his studio also pulled some strings. They made combat movies instead of actual combat. If you're only ever playing the character of you, when do you start to believe your own scripts?

DUKE: Some words can give you a warm feeling.

AUTHOR: When does the individual memory become the fact? Was I even at the hospital in November of 1979?

REAGAN: In spite of the wildly speculative and false stories of arms for hostages and alleged ransom payments, we did not—repeat *did not*—trade weapons or anything else for hostages, nor will we.

AUTHOR: What do we have to do to save ourselves from our enemies? From ourselves?

REAGAN: A few months ago, I told the American people I did not trade arms for hostages. My heart and my best intentions still tell me that's true, but the facts and evidence tell me it is not.

DUKE: Half of you men throw up a barricade here, throw up a barricade. Go to the north wall! (*From upstage, a bayonet stabs him. He stumbles off and we hear a sound like a powder magazine explosion. Some dust clouds spread on stage.*)

AUTHOR: What's his legacy? The resurgence of conservatives? The debt? A military-industrial complex? We're still nervous about Russia. We're still trying to figure out Iran. We still have all these bombs all over the country, any of which could get loose. Sometimes these days, I think about Mutually Assured Destruction or nuclear winter, and sometimes I stand on the National Mall or in midtown Manhattan and think about a suitcase or a car trunk and what could fit inside it.

DUKE re-enters, noticeably older, dressed as a cattle driver, red bandanna around his neck.

DUKE: Summer's over.

AUTHOR: Is it? I wonder if we're getting better or worse. I can't tell.

DUKE: You're a pretty independent character, aren't you?

REAGAN: After two hundred years, the centuries, she still stands strong and true to the granite ridge, and her glow has held no matter what storm. And she's still a beacon, still a magnet for all who must have freedom, for all the pilgrims from all the lost places who are hurtling through the darkness, toward here.

AUTHOR: I'm at an age when my fears no longer feel irrational. I worry about what's next, what's to be done to help the future. I don't have kids, but I think about what happens next anyway.

Several shots from behind hit DUKE. He collapses to the floor.

DUKE: I'm proud of you. All of you. Every man wants his children to be better than he was. You are. (*Lights down on him*)

AUTHOR: John Wayne died on screen in just seven movies. Reagan only played a bad guy a handful of times. In movies, you get rehearsals, second takes, third takes, more. Edit booths. If a narrative gets tough, you dissolve to the next scene. The real world is different. Right?

DUKE re-enters. He looks very old. We notice, too, that REAGAN has also aged. Maybe, too, the AUTHOR. What happened to the crowd? Where did they go?

DUKE: We all have our time.

AUTHOR: Anyone can be president, we tell ourselves. Really, though, not even four dozen men over a couple hundred years. That's it. That's the movie we've been watching.

REAGAN: I now begin the journey that will lead me into the sunset of my life.

DUKE: This is my birthday. Gimme the best in the house. Thank you, sir. (*Four bullets strike him from off stage. He collapses. Lights down on him.*)

AUTHOR: I don't remember it happening this way. (*Lights down on him.*)

REAGAN: I know that for America there will always be a bright dawn ahead.

FADE OUT—*THE END.*

Box Score

George H. W. Bush
Forty-first President of the United States
1989-1993
202 years since the Constitution
126 years since Emancipation
15 years since the resignation

He is left-handed, perfect for first base, the edge of his foot on the bag while he stretches out his lanky frame for the ball that comes to him from the infield. When his Yale teammates throw, it is perfect, Ivy League quality, a searing bit of whiteness that does not lazily arc through the sky but rather buzzes, high-pitched, an angry insect that the flytrap of his glove will close upon. It is perfect for him to use his body this way, this clean movement of muscle. When he was a pilot in the war, he bailed out of a burning airplane, his parachute jerking his body as he fell to Earth. This is better, to use his body this way.

It is 1990. The war gets further away every day. He played in the first two College World Series, although Yale lost both times. Part of his job now is to throw out a first pitch every year, to officially open the professional season; Taft started this, with his corpulence so different from George's own body. George is a sportsman; the body doesn't forget. But he was a first baseman, not a pitcher; he is used to collecting the ball, not throwing it, the double play ends with him, Tinker to Evers to Bush.

He throws out a first pitch in Canada this year, at the new stadium. He meets with their prime minister, for talks (their official reason), but he is there for the baseball, for the chance to be on the field again.

In 1948, after his return from the war, he played ball at Yale, captain of the team, a war hero now taking a different kind of field. As captain,

136

he led the team, represented them when they needed a representative, and so it fell to him to meet with Babe Ruth when the greatest player in the world donated the manuscript of his memoir to Yale.

The two met on the field in New Haven. George, a wiry frame under baggy pinstripes, leans forward slightly to accept the manuscript from Ruth, smartly dressed in a suit. Just two months later, Ruth would die in a cancer ward.

His voice was already ravaged a year earlier, when he spoke at Babe Ruth Day at Yankee Stadium. To an adoring crowd, he spoke briefly—*You know how bad my voice sounds, well, it feels just as bad*—into a mic from WABD.

This baseball game of ours comes up from the youth, he tells them, the voice crackling from a throat riddled with cancer. *That means the boys.*

The boys, like the ones at Yale he'll meet next year. Many of them, like their captain, might as well be men already; they've fought in a war, come back to marry the girls they left behind, even started a family—when George comes home from the games, he might kiss Barbara on the cheek, lift up little George W. from his crib.

Ruth: *After you're a boy and grow up to know how to play ball, then you come to the boys you see representing themselves today in your national pastime.*

George does so much. He moves to Texas, sells drilling equipment, and then drills the Permian Basin himself. He gets himself elected a Congressman, votes to abolish the draft, advocates for birth control so fervently that his colleagues nickname him "Rubbers," runs for the Senate and loses. Then he's United Nations Ambassador, Republican National Committee chair, Special Liaison to China, Director of Central Intelligence, presidential candidate, vice president, then president. Think about the ball whipping from player to player, Bush is the utility man, able to play any position, take any stance you need him to.

Gray-haired Ruth leans into the mic: *And if you're successful, and you try hard enough, you're bound to come out on top—just like these boys have come to the top now.*

In a few months, Yale and its first baseman will play in the championship series for the first-ever College World Series. In a year, less than three weeks after George accepts the manuscript from Ruth, Yale plays again for the title.

They lose both years.

Ruth said that baseball was *the only real game, I think, in the world.*

In 1990, George wears a Texas Rangers jacket, the team his son owns. He grins broadly when stepping onto the field, lighter and happier than his Canadian counterpart. He points to his catcher, calling the pitch, snaps it off while the prime minister is setting himself. The form is still there, the drawing back, the following through, the ball leaving his hand as simply and cleanly as the SkyDome's retractable roof (which is not retracted).

How little time remains for George to do this. Just twice more before he is called out, retired by the rookie from Arkansas. It's a pitcher/first baseman play, to try to pick off the runner on first. *Caught him napping*, the announcers say.

But that day in Toronto, under the roof, all that is far ahead of him. George is pure joy at this moment, an old man at the top of his game, a young man remembering his game. As they interview him in a suite later, the crowd will roar at the action on the field. He'll hear it, crook his thumb over his shoulder toward the noise; *I like all that*, he'll say, the grin again. All that, the greatest game, he thinks, in the world.

Letter from Oxford

William J. Clinton
Forty-second President of the United States
1993-2001
206 years since the Constitution
130 years since the Emancipation
19 years since the resignation

There is a lot that I could say about him, the first president to have an e-mail address, the second president to be impeached, the five-term governor of Arkansas. Enough miles of columns to cover the road from Hope to Little Rock to Washington to Harlem to Chappaqua and back. I could write about his failure to intervene in Rwanda and ask if the president has a moral responsibility to the world. I could write about a White House intern and ask if the president has a moral responsibility to himself. I could write about walking into a voting booth at age twenty, my first time voting in a presidential election, and seeing his name on the ballot against my longtime senator.

Instead, there's a letter he wrote a long time ago, when he was just a little older than I was when I filled in an oval. He was twenty-three in 1969. He knew who he was supposed to be, and what he had to do, and more importantly not do, to become it.

A quick history lesson: presidents have fought in every officially declared war, with three—Monroe, Hayes, and Bush senior—wounded in combat. For most of this country's existence, a spell in a uniform was a means by which a man could become electable, and in some cases—Taylor, Grant, Eisenhower—it was pretty much all the experience we needed to put them in the bully pulpit.

Then there was a war, never officially declared but a war nonetheless, in Southeast Asia. The first name inscribed into the black granite wall of the Vietnam Veterans Memorial died in 1959, the last name in 1975. Sixteen years in Vietnam, and it nearly—perhaps did—tear this country apart.

Here's a thing to try: when you meet men of a certain age, ask them their draft number. They all remember it.

That war changed us in so many ways as a country, and one of them is how we thought about military service. The three men of the Baby Boomer generation who have been president all found a way not to go—bone spurs or National Guard or arranging to join the ROTC—and the three veterans who ran for president all lost; in Kerry's case, his service even became a liability. Something shifted.

Back to specifics: Oxford, the end of the '60s. Bill Clinton, in his second year as a Rhodes Scholar, has received a deferment, 2-S, for his studies at that august institution, but time is running out on his two years, and when he returns to Arkansas the next year, he will be eligible for the draft (1-A) at a time when the United States is feeding young men by the tens of thousands into Vietnam.

He is not the kind of young man who has a father who can arrange something, some semblance of service without the risk. So he does what he can, and after failing to find something in the National Guard or the Air Force, he secures himself a spot in the University of Arkansas's ROTC program, with some help from a senator (he is no fortunate son, but he is a Rhodes Scholar, and that's not without its advantages). He receives a 1-D classification.

All this time, he is protesting the war on Oxford's campus, marching against it, organizing protests. He considers it an immoral war, something to stand up against, and he's not alone. In 1969, the country is split on the war. The previous year's Tet Offensive showed that Hanoi would not succumb under the tremendous numbers of the U.S., and that no matter how many dead and wounded and destroyed the military reported, it didn't seem to be enough to win. Nixon promises "an honorable end" to the war when he campaigns for the presidency the year prior, and marches both for and against the war fill the streets.

Clinton makes all these arrangements—nothing illegal, but arrangements that will raise questions nonetheless—and then he decides not to go through with it, to enter the draft. Bill Clinton draws a high draft number, 311. He won't go, not unless the war elevates drastically. He no longer needs that ROTC slot.

Bill Clinton is twenty-three years old in 1969. Apollo XII has returned from the moon and the Beatles are recording their final songs. JFK, whom the young Clinton pushed his way toward during a White House visit, has been dead and gone for six years. MLK and RFK are gone too, to assassins' bullets. These are the days the Boomers will remember, their summers of love and eves of destruction.

Dear Colonel Holmes, I am sorry to be so long in writing, he writes to the colonel with whom he's corresponded, who helped him get into the ROTC. His apology comes because he has spent a long time thinking *about what I want to and ought to say.*

As you know, I worked for two years in a very minor position on the Senate Foreign Relations Committee, he writes. *I did it for the experience and the salary, but also for the opportunity, however small, of working every day against a war I opposed and despised with a depth of feeling I had reserved solely for racism in America before Vietnam.*

What he wants to say and what he ought to say: this is the central contradiction of Bill Clinton. The id and the superego, desire and duty, feeling and thinking. But it goes beyond that simple duality to something more complicated, something that might explain him and us and America and all the contradictions of this country, how we could hold ourselves to lofty standards that we constantly fall short of.

He takes Colonel Holmes through the evolution of his thinking, from his research on Vietnam to how that relates to the draft, to his decision that *no government really rooted in limited, parliamentary democracy should have the power to make its citizens fight and kill and die in a war they may oppose, a war which even possibly may be wrong, a war which, in any case, does not involve immediately the peace and freedom of the nation.*

He discusses two friends at Oxford, conscientious objectors, and his roommate, a draft resister, who may be indicted and may be barred from the United States, even though *he is one of the bravest, best men I know. His country needs men like him more than they know. That he is considered a criminal is an obscenity.*

We can read the incremental steps of his logic—here is the situation, here are the abstract ideas behind it, here are examples of how people have reacted to it—and we can see the next step coming forward: here is how it applies to him.

He admits the difficulty of it, calling the decision *the most difficult of my life.* But why? What changed his mind and made him decide to submit his name for this war that he has fought against for so long?

I decided to accept the draft in spite of my beliefs for one reason: to maintain my political viability within the system. For years I have worked to prepare myself for a political life characterized by both practical political ability and concern for rapid social progress. It is a life I still feel compelled to try to lead.

He is twenty-three years old, a time of transition. He will return to the United States, go to Yale for law school, meet his future wife there. He makes this decision because he knows who he is supposed to be.

Perhaps belief is destiny, and what Bill Clinton is able to do at twenty-three, to find a way into the ROTC because it is *the one way left in which I could possibly, but not positively, avoid both Vietnam and resistance,* because he understands the impossibility of that war and his goals. He sees that the times are changing, and that the path to the presidency will not, at least for him, run through a boot camp.

Eight years later, he'll become the youngest governor in Arkansas history, and two years later, the youngest ex-governor. He'll find a way back to the governor's mansion in Little Rock and occupy it until he moves into the White House, where we find ourselves regarding the often-asked questions (the intern, Rwanda, Bosnia, NAFTA, Waco, OKC, eliminating the budget deficit) once more.

The particulars of my personal life are not nearly as important to me as the principles involved, he wrote in that letter, the cold December of Oxford outside the window. He knows, as he writes it, that he will not go into the heat of Saigon, that someone else will go.

This young man, in some ways still a boy, in other ways fully grown, will finish his letter to Colonel Holmes. In twenty-eight years, he'll normalize diplomatic relations between the United States and

Vietnam. Tonight, though, he will close with *forgive the length of this letter. There was much to say. There is still a lot to be said, but it can wait. Please say hello to Colonel Jones for me. Merry Christmas.*
    Sincerely, Bill Clinton.

In my first presidential election, in 1996, I voted for Bill Clinton. The principles of his personal life were not nearly as important to me as the particulars. In 1992, when Ted Koppel dedicated an episode of *Nightline* to interviewing Clinton about this, the then-governor said *We've been talking about a letter I wrote twenty-two years ago as if it's a test of present presidential character.*

    Was it? I suppose it depends, as he said years later in a much different conversation, it depends what your definition of *is* is.

Evacuation Route

George W. Bush
Forty-third President of the United States
2001-2009
214 years since the Constitution
138 years since Emancipation
27 years since the resignation

Category One: This is the face of a man who has lost the script. Card enters the classroom, interrupts the reading of *My Pet Goat*, whispers in his ear: *A second plane, a second tower.* You could argue that his expression at that moment is stoic, but look closely at his small eyes—he realizes the hurricane is coming. He realizes he is in over his head. He realizes he may drown.

Category Two: He surfaces in New York City, wearing a warrior's face. He stands, armed with a bullhorn, future artifact, on top of the pile. *I can hear you,* he says. A few days later: *Wanted, dead or alive.* I remember reading a first responder writing in these days, *There's nothing here but dust and rebar.*

Category Three: To say the storm is gathering is wrong. The storm is already here. His father, twelve years earlier, said *The world could wait no longer.* Now he wears his father's face, announces the same war, the same target. I watch a television set up on a folding table in the middle of a mall in the Midwest, the security guard and the late movie audience rapt. I don't know the meaning of *Fallujah* or *IED* yet. Neither does my friend, a Navy medic. We'll learn, in different ways.

Category Four: This is the face of victory, but why look at the face? There's so much happening—the landing, the flight suit, the aircraft carrier (the *Abraham Lincoln*—you'll want to find irony in this, but it's empty—Lincoln knew how to wage war, knew sometimes you have to suspend habeas corpus). Soldiers get a deck of cards, the fifty-two most-wanted, Saddam the ace of spades. Look at the president's face, here on the deck of the *Abraham Lincoln*. His is not the face of a joker; he is the card in the new pack that explains the rules of the game, the one you want to throw away but can't.

Category Five: During him, the storm. He is Louis XV, Katrina his Madame de Pompadour, a helicopter ride over New Orleans their legacy. I am projecting here, but when I look at him looking at the drowned city, I see his face remembering the Florida classroom almost four years earlier, the whisper in the ear, the overwhelming tides moving toward him too quickly. When I see his face, I see also the joker's face as Kanye states *George W. Bush doesn't care about black people*, panic washing over him, the flood again and again. He serves two terms, eight years, but really, it's just these four, an early September to a late August, a rise and a fall, a cresting and ebbing, mud and rebar. In the next three years, it will all slip under. My navy medic friend will be put under the ground. Finally, on a cold January day, Bush will go up, another ride in a helicopter, leaving Washington behind as his successor parades down Pennsylvania Avenue. As he flies away, the crowd will sing: *Na na / hey hey hey / goodbye*. And his face, which has seen so much over these eight years, has seen the states turn blue and red and start to drift apart, has seen towers fall and a city drown, this face that has aged in front of us through so much change—what does his face look like then?

What They Said About Him

Barack Obama
Forty-fourth President of the United States
2009-2017
222 years since the Constitution
146 years since Emancipation
35 years since the resignation

Have we had a president like him before? The easy grace, the timeless cool, the effortlessness of the three-point shot dropping in the basket. First, the young candidate for Senate on the convention stage charming the faithful, then four years later the stadium full as he accepts the nomination, and in five months he stands in the bright cold and takes the oath—when in our lives had we seen that? The differences were obvious, the differences went beyond the surface—we'd never had a president like him before.

We'd never had a president like him before, the focal point of a white-hot rage flooding every channel, tea kettles of minds continuously at the boil, the outrage never stopping, the coded language we didn't need an Enigma to understand: *Thug. Monkey.* The ways they used his middle name as an insult, Barack *Hussein* Obama, the way they turned the answers into more questions for their fires, the way they found their echo chambers in cable networks and 140 characters, how the resonances grew to stadium-level noises. We'd had characters before him—the Fool, the Philanderer, the Wimp—but we had not seen this before.

Had we seen a president like this before? Over the hills of Afghanistan, a predator flies nonstop, scanning the landscape. Eight years prior, we had bumper stickers that replaced Endless War with End this War, and what did we get for our efforts? We supported our troops by replacing them with machines. Remember that April night when the networks said that the president would make a statement?

Remember watching the static live shot of the podium, the red carpet of the long hallway? Remember him finally appearing, the walk to the podium? All our answers just seem to raise more questions. All our solutions just seem to create more problems, both the same and different from before.

Had we seen a president like him before? Every Democrat since Truman tried and failed to reform health care. In a year, he turned a nightmare recession into continued job growth. He worked on pay inequality, signed arms treaties, improved school lunches. When, in his second inaugural, he mentioned "Seneca Falls, and Selma, and Stonewall," didn't your throat catch? When he paused while speaking in Charleston, then sang "Amazing Grace," the crowd cheering and joining, had you ever heard that before?

Did anyone ever see the president we thought we elected? What happened to the reformer? What happened to the crusader? The rich got richer, the banks got stronger, the dollars seemed to flow in one direction, only up. All those fears from the right—*He'll redistribute wealth, he'll take our guns*—never came to fruition. Were we better off than we were eight years ago? All those opportunities lost, all those chances wasted. Did we progress with a progressive in office, or did it seem like we just ran hard enough to stay in the same place?

They had never seen a president like him before, and now the absolute terror of what will follow in his wake—the door thrown open wide to white nationalists. Their song of sealing the borders—that will echo for quite some time. They heard someone say *Black lives matter*, and they responded with *No, all lives matter*, and it's possible to draw a line from that to some of them chanting *Jews will not replace us* in Charlottesville. When they said *I just want my country back*, they meant *from him* but also *from them* and *from you*. Part of his legacy is that the party of Lincoln threw itself into the hands of the paranoid and furious. The party that freed the slaves became the party that remembered the slave uprisings, and now their fears guide them into unfamiliar territories, lands with strange costumes, strange buildings, a leader they've never seen before because their leaders have always looked like them.

Have I ever seen a president like him before? I've never seen a president at all, but him I heard in a small town in Virginia during the first campaign. Tens of thousands of people crowding the campus circle, waiting through the rain—the biggest thing to happen in that town since the Civil War, since Lincoln visited—and we couldn't get close enough to see the stage. In the press of our fellow citizens, we heard the cheers go up as the candidate stepped on stage. How did he look? I've seen photos—no jacket, white sleeves rolled up. A light rain falling. But I didn't see him at that time. The first debate had been the night before. I remember he said, "You know, John McCain had a lot to say about me last night, but he didn't have a lot to say about you." We cheered. We'd never heard a candidate like him before.

Nomenclature

Donald Trump
Forty-fifth President of the United States
2017-tbd
230 years since the Constitution
154 years since Emancipation
43 years since the resignation

Adam gave all the animals different names, but Trump gives everything the same name—his. A tower in midtown Manhattan, another on Wall Street, another in Chicago. Hotels around the world, including one in the old Post Office building on Pennsylvania Avenue in Washington, just blocks from the White House. He has, in the past, put his name on a university, a steaks-by-mail company, a casino in New Jersey. He has put his name on three wives, five children, an administration, an era.

Usually, the presidency makes a name. Certainly, we have elected famous men with name recognition before—Eisenhower, Reagan— just as we have elected wealthy men before. But their names were affixed to buildings and street signs after their time in office, not before. Trump is not that way. He existed as personality before we understood him as president. He is brand, he is corporate and incorporated. He is without boundaries in an office designed to be checked by two other branches, iconoclastic in a house full of icons. He is not *out of many, one*; he is *out of one, more of that one*. He is a copy machine, a cloning device, a rubber stamp dedicated to the same thing over and over and over: *Trump Trump Trump Trump Trump.*

The presidency has been bigger than the person occupying the office, until Trump. We used to speak of the office and the holder of the office as separate things, talked about how we expected certain behaviors and pronouncements from the officeholder, because they were the president, and that's what a president did.

Trump is Trump, who is also president. Before his inauguration, some wondered if he might be changed by the gravitas of the office, the way that others had been.

Now it seems that the accurate thing to say is that while Trump has not been changed by the presidency, the presidency has most assuredly been changed by Trump.

Let us engage in a failure of the imagination: the idea that he might have been created by the office he swore to execute. That Donald J. Trump, Manhattan real estate mogul and television personality, sits in the chair behind the Resolute Desk in the Oval Office on his first day in office and recognizes the gravity of the situation, the forces at work. "I alone can fix it," he said on the convention stage, but imagine that he now realizes that his name is not enough to do this work, that he needs others, not just family and a few trusted advisors, but a large team of staff and government workers. Imagine that he looks out upon the swamp he railed against in the campaign and realizes that it teems with life, a vast ecosystem. Imagine that he uses his Twitter account and its millions of followers as a way to communicate effectively to the American people, something beyond the instant gratification of his base.

The presidency, and with it America, is based on an idea of continuity. Power passes from term and term and party to party without violence or revolution. Trump has disrupted that in the way that businessmen often laud. He has given the presidency his name, rather than taken on its title.

Vineyards, hotels, golf courses: he gives his name to things, but I was wrong to say that he only gives his name. He gives lots of names: *Lyin' Hillary, Sleepy Joe, Crazy Nancy, Low Energy Jeb, Slimeball James Comey, Dumb as a Rock AOC, Little Marco, Shifty Schiff, Pocahontas, Low-IQ Maxine Waters, the China Virus.* Those he likes still get his name: the president of Mexico becomes "Juan Trump," the prime minister of Great Britain "Britain Trump." He makes his creations into his image. Names are power. What's in a name?

He is impeached, and he is acquitted. One senator stated that "the question then is not whether the president did it, but whether the

United States Senate or the American people should decide what to do about what he did." In other words, what name will you put to this? High crimes? Distraction? Treason? Harassment? Witch hunt? What's in a name? Everything. Everything.

A New York State Park on land he gave. A settlement in the Golan Heights named in recognition of his support of Israel's claim. He gives his name, an act of charity, an act of connection. The father of all mankind, the benevolent bestowal, a legacy passed on and on and on, echoing through the years. Look on his works. Nothing else remains.

The number of baby boys named Donald has decreased steadily since 2015.

Enfranchisement

Forty-___th President of the United States
20__-20__
2__ years since the Constitution
1__ years since Emancipation
4_ years since the resignation

WASHINGTON—_____was inaugurated as the forty-sixth president of the United States on _____, promising the American people that the new president would "_____."

  In a ceremony that included _____, President _____ presented a vision of an America _____ by "_____" of _____ and _____, requiring _____.

  "I will _____," _____ told admirers and onlookers in an Inaugural Address from the West Front of the Capitol. "_____."

  _____'s inauguration was marked by _____. The election, which was_____, resulted in _____.

  "In conclusion, _____" President _____ continued, "_____."

Instructions to Citizens: Please fill out this form using blue or black ink. Be sure to fill in each blank completely. As you fill out the form, consider the form of a representative democracy, in which citizens vote for their representatives. Remember the slow, painful work it took to expand that democracy: the suffragettes in prison, the marchers on the Edmund Pettus bridge, the endless lines to cast a ballot. Consider this whole experiment in people, how much faith we place in the fallible. Do not fold, spindle, or mutilate this form. Show your work.

Amendment: Last Dance

When we inaugurate a new president, we hold a dance to celebrate. The president talks, then he walks, and then he dances with his wife for the nation.

I find this very charming. Perhaps because of the quaintness of it, how it seems like a holdover from a quieter time in America. Perhaps because I have never voted for a president based on the idea of how good a dancer he might be, and yet it is one of the first things he performs publicly. Perhaps because I love the idea of George and Martha Washington, tall and short, dancing together, and there is an echo of that mismatched harmony of the first couple in the new First Couple as they dance, an intermission between the acts.

The Virginia Reel that George and Martha danced originated in Scotland. It took us a long time to create an American dance. We are still figuring out the steps.

I was born in the year of the Bicentennial, in a year of celebration. When I was a baby, the tall ships sailed into the bay, past the Statue of Liberty, past the twin towers, themselves only a few years old. President Ford declared that the bells of America should ring for two minutes at two o'clock on July 4, in commemoration of two hundred years of independence.

I assume that this happened, and that, at three months old, I heard the bells of Mission, Kansas, pealing for those two minutes. At that age, I would react to loud sounds and recognize my mother's voice. I would be on the cusp of paying attention to music. I had not yet learned how to distinguish the signal from the noise.

In an address he made in Philadelphia on the Fourth of July, Gerald Ford said that "it is right that Americans are always improving. It is not only right, it is necessary." The nation had emerged from its biggest constitutional crisis since the Civil War only two years earlier; it was still figuring out the signal from the noise.

The name for a 250th anniversary is a sestercentennial or a semiquincentennial. Neither term is an easy one, but I suppose we will learn how to say it. The planning is underway in Philadelphia, where we celebrated the centennial, sesquicentennial, and bicentennial. They will plant trees and bury a time capsule and host baseball's All-Star Game. In other cities and states, they are making plans, forming committees, resolving to study the matter.

These celebrations seem to follow upon national traumas—the internal strife of the Civil War, the slaughter of the First World War, the betrayal of Watergate. The semiquincentennial will occur in the wake of a time when we have frequently discussed the lack of civility in politics, seen a rise in nationalism at home and abroad, and lamented the division in our culture. Perhaps acknowledging our two hundred and fiftieth year of existence will help us to reunite. Perhaps not.

In October of 1976, President Ford awarded choreographer Martha Graham the Presidential Medal of Freedom, the nation's highest honor for a civilian. Graham, then seventy-eight years old, had developed a style of dance that broke from the European traditions, working with American composers and American dancers to create an American dance, one that expressed our emotions and passions and tragedies. She taught generations of dancers, including a girl from Michigan named Betty Bloomer, who, in 1976, clapped as her husband placed the medal around Graham's neck.

Decades earlier, Graham had said that "dance is communication, and the great desire is to speak clearly and beautifully and with inevitability." Now, with the blue ribbon of the Medal of Freedom on her, she cited an old saying: "They had no poet, so they died."

"In other words," she said, "the city, the country, had no one to sing, or to dance their imagination, their dreams, and their faith, so they disappeared from the memory of man. And I would like to feel that those of us who are dancers have contributed toward a singing voice that will go on for a long time."

By the time Ford awarded Graham, the creator of modern dance, American dance, the Medal of Freedom, I could communicate using gestures, like waving or holding my arms up. In a way, I had learned to use my body to communicate.

The dance can become a kind of fever, sometimes. We can't stop doing it, no matter our level of exhaustion. Shouldn't we stop before we collapse? Before our feet give out from underneath us? What keeps us going? Tradition, the notion that is what was done before us? ("You got a price to pay just like anybody else!" yelled one American to another during a Vietnam War protest.)

Or do we dance because we think of perfection, of more perfect unions? As Ford said, "the American adventure is a continuous process. As one milestone is passed, another is sighted." As Graham said, "the dancer is realistic. His craft teaches him to be. Either the foot is pointed, or it is not. No amount of dreaming will point it for you."

Do we drop the metaphors and continue this because we still believe in Graham's idea of the dancer as a "divine normal"? After so long, I wonder if we remember the first notes of the song, the first steps of the dance anymore, or it's all vanished, like the exposition buildings of 1876 and 1926, like the wakes of the tall ships in 1976.

Born that year, I grew up in a city in the heart of the country. I was a Boy Scout and student council president. I danced, awkwardly, in church basements and school cafeterias where the lights had been dimmed and vending machines wrapped in aluminum foil to create an atmosphere. I danced when the gym teacher rolled a record player onto the floor and taught us square dancing. I danced in clubs and at wedding receptions, and I danced alone in my room when I could think of no other way to respond to the music I heard.

I tried to speak clearly, and beautifully, and with inevitability, and I chose forty-four men as dance partners, sailing in and out of the harbor, watching how they led the steps of their partners from point to point.

Again, I marvel over how odd it is that one of the first things we see a new president do is dance. How strange to see them in this physical task when what we have asked them to do is so thoroughly cerebral.

Dances end with a return to the start. Think again of George Washington, the false teeth, the towering stature. Once, in a library in the nation's capital, I requested a document from the librarian in their vaults. After a few minutes, she brought it out to me, placing a box on the table.

"Try not to touch it too much," she said, and walked away.

Puzzled, I opened the box and found an ordinary manila folder. Inside were four sheets of paper, a letter written by Washington declining an honorary position, explaining that he was much too busy with Mount Vernon and his retirement to participate.

I held the letter, carefully, the same sheets of paper that Washington himself had held. No plastic protected the pages, and I felt the frisson of history running through me. It felt electric. It felt alive. I felt like dancing.

Notes

This book began because I realized two things in the summer of 2009: first, I couldn't name all the presidents in order, and second, there were forty-four months until the next presidential election. If I read a presidential biography each month, then I could have them all read by the time the next election came around. The list of books I've read since then is in the Appendix; the basic biographical facts of each president, in large part, come from them.

1   **I do solemnly swear**: Article II, Section 1, Constitution of the United States of America.

one of the nineteen museums: "The Smithsonian offers eleven museums and galleries on the National Mall plus six other museums and the National Zoo in the greater National Capital Area. In New York City, we invite you to tour two museums in historic settings." https://www.si.edu/museums.

4   **George Washington loved to dance**: Philip G. Smucker, "Washington on the Dance Floor," https://www.mountvernon.org/george-washington/athleticism/on-the-dance-floor/.

first in war, first in peace: taken from Henry Lee's eulogy of Washington.

the 6-foot, 2-inch, 175-pound George Washington: Joseph Ellis, *His Excellency* (New York: Alfred A. Knopf, 2004).

He danced for hours with his generals' wives: Smucker, "Washington on the Dance Floor."

barely five feet: "Ten Facts about Martha Washington," https://www.mountvernon.org/george-washington/martha-washington/ten-facts-about-martha-washington/.

5   **Building X, they call it**: Seth C. Bruggeman, *Here, George Washington Was Born: Memory, Material Culture, and the Public History of a National Monument* (Athens: University of Georgia Press, 2008).

At the farm, they had only found: John Noble Wilford, "Archeologists Agree: Young Washington Slept Here," *New York Times*, July 3, 2008, A15.

crockery with a cherry tree motif: Mara Katkins, Melanie Marquis, Ruth Ann Armitage, and Daniel Fraser, "Mary Washington's Mended Ceramics: A Study of Eighteenth-Century Glues," *Ceramics in America*, 2016. http://www.chipstone.org/article.php/743/Ceramics-in-America-2016/Mary-Washington's-Mended-Ceramics:-A-Study-of-Eighteenth-Century-Glues

6   **copying his own set of rules**: "The Rules of Civility," https://www. mountvernon.org/george-washington/rules-of-civility/

Even the false teeth: Colin Schultz, "George Washington Didn't Have Wooden Teeth: They Were Ivory," https://www.smithsonianmag.com/ smart-news/george-washington-didnt-have-wooden-teeth-they-were-ivory-180953273/.

7   **dances could go all night**: Smucker, "Washington on the Dance Floor."

some of his officers: Robert F. Haggard, "The Nicola Affair: Lewis Nicola, George Washington, and American Military Discontent During the Revolutionary War," *Proceedings of the American Philosophical Society*, Vol. 146, No. 2 (June 2002), 139-69.

In reading stories of the presidents: See the Appendix for a full list.

His beloved Marquis: Hank Parfitt, "Lafayette and Slavery," https:// www.lafayettesociety.org/lafayette-and-slavery/

he brought his slaves with him: Erin Blakemore, "George Washington Used Legal Loopholes to Avoid Freeing His Slaves," https://www. smithsonianmag.com/smart-news/george-washington-used-legal-loopholes-avoid-freeing-his-slaves-180954283/.

privately supported gradual emancipation: "Washington's Changing Views on Slavery," https://www.mountvernon.org/george-washington/ slavery/washingtons-   changing-views-on-slavery/

He freed his slaves: "A Decision to Free His Slaves," https://www. mountvernon.org/george-washington/slavery/washingtons-1799-will/

Martha owned many more: Ibid.

8   **zero milestone**: Richard F. Weingroff, "Zero Milestone – Washington, DC," https://www.fhwa.dot.gov/infrastructure/zero.cfm.

Here is a man: "Washington's Slave List, June 1799," https://founders. archives.gov/documents/Washington/06-04-02-0405.

10   **loves pomp and circumstance**: For example, Adams proposed that the president have the title "His Highness, the President of the United States and Protector of Their Liberties." We went with "Mr. President" instead. James H. Huston, "John Adams' Title Campaign," *New England Quarterly*, Vol. 41, No. 1 (March 1968), 30-39.

11   **then a single book**: *John Adams*, by David McCullough, who had previously   rehabilitated Harry Truman's reputation in a biography published in 1992.

that name itself has faded: Mary Lynn Ritzenthaler and Catherine Nicholson, "The Declaration of Independence and the Hand of Time," *Prologue*, Vol. 48, No. 3 (Fall   2016). https://www.archives.gov/publications/prologue/2016/fall/declaration.

12   **how they claim**: "Spurious Quotations," https://www.monticello.org/site/research-and-collections/spurious-quotations.

"dusky Sally": Philip Kennicott, "Sally Hemings Gets Her Recognition at Monticello," *Washington Post*, June 17, 2018. https://www.washingtonpost.com/entertainment/museums/jeffersons-monticello-finally-gives-sally-hemings-her-place-in-presidential-history/2018/06/12/55145ac0-6504-11e8-a69c-b944de66d9e7_story.html.

homemade Bible: the Bible was on display in the Albert Small Documents Gallery of the National Museum of American History from November 2011 to July 2012. https://americanhistory.si.edu/exhibitions/jefferson-bible.

keeping watch for the wooly mammoth: Technically, the mastodon, but Jefferson   thought they were mammoths. Cara Giaimo, "Thomas Jefferson Built This Country on Mastodons," *Atlas Obscura*, https://www.atlasobscura.com/articles/thomas-jefferson-built-this-country-on-mastodons.

your declaration under bulletproof glass: The bulletproof nature of the glass isn't quite confirmed. The conventional wisdom is that the glass is bulletproof, but the National Institute of Standards and Technology, who built the current cases, states that it is not. A glass industry blog claims that a layer of polycarbonate material between the glass and the document is what protects the Declaration from bullets. This is endlessly fascinating to me. Please see: "Preserving Our Nation's Watchwords: The Charters of Freedom Encasements," https://www.nist.gov/nist-time-capsule/making-nist-case-preservation/preserving-our-nations-watchwords-charters-freedom; and "Bulletproof Glass and the Declaration of Independence," https://glassdoctor.com/blog/bulletproof-glass-and-the-declaration-of-independence.

13   **painted words of accusation**: Grace Bird, "Jefferson Statue Vandalized at Virginia," *Inside Higher Ed*, April 16, 2018. https://www.insidehighered.com/quicktakes/2018/04/16/jefferson-statue-vandalized-virginia.

there is a memorial for a young woman: John Garza, "Heather Hayer's mother visits memorial on one-year anniversary of daughter's death," *Cavalier Daily*, August 12, 2018. https://www.cavalierdaily.com/article/2018/08/heather-heyers-mother-visits-memorial-on-one-year-anniversary-of-daughters-death.

opened up a Native burial ground: Jeffrey Hantman, "Jefferson's Mound Archeological Site," *Encyclopedia Virginia*, https://www.encyclopediavirginia.org/Jefferson_s_Mound_Archaeological_Site.

wall of separation: The phrase famously appears in Jefferson's 1802 letter to the Danbury Baptists, https://www.loc.gov/loc/lcib/9806/danpre.html

Kennedy said: "Extract from John F. Kennedy's Remarks at a Dinner Honoring Nobel Prize Winners of the Western Hemisphere," http://tjrs. monticello.org/letter/1856.

14   **Those who stay behind will save a few things**: Thomas Fleming, "When Dolley   Madison Took Command of the White House," https://www.smithsonianmag.com/history/how-dolley-madison-saved-the-day-7465218/.

finally emancipated: "The Life of Paul Jennings," https://www.mont-pelier.org/learn/paul-jennings.

15   **Madison evacuates early**: Fleming, "When Dolley Madison Took Command."

led by Sir George Cockburn: Caleb Crain, "Unfortunate Events," *New Yorker*, October 15, 2012.

she instructs the servants: Fleming, "When Dolley Madison Took Command."

breaking the frame: Ibid.

wondering at divine intervention: Sarah Zielinski, "The Tornado that Saved Washington." https://www.smithsonianmag.com/science-nature/the-tornado-that-saved-   washington-33901211/.

works as Madison's valet: "The Life of Paul Jennings."

16   **plans a slave revolt**: Elizabeth Dowling Taylor, "Paul Jennings," *Encyclopedia Virginia*, https://www.encyclopediavirginia.org/Jennings_Paul_1799-1874.

the first White House memoir: Paul Jennings, *A Colored Man's Reminiscences of James Madison* (Brooklyn: George C. Beadle, 1865).

almost two hundred years: Rachel L. Swarns, "Madison and the White House, Through   the Memoir of a Slave," New York Times, August 16, 2009, A12.

Scent is the sense closest to memory: Ashley Hamer, "Here's Why Smells Trigger Such Vivid Memories," https://www.discovery.com/science/Why-Smells-Trigger-Such-Vivid-Memories.

17   **In *On Photography***: Susan Sontag, *On Photography* (New York: Farrar, Straus and   Giroux, 1977).

only in the 1820s does a Frenchman: On display at the Harry Ransom Center at the University of Texas. "The Niépce Heliograph." https://www.hrc.utexas.edu/niepce-   heliograph/.

Louis Daguerre announced: Ibid.

the first two humans photographed: Ian Jeffery, *The Photography Book*, 2nd ed. (New York City: Phaidon Press, 2014).

18   **John Vanderlyn's portrait**: "James Monroe." https://npg.si.edu/object/npg_NPG.70.59

People line up to take their picture: Sarah Cascone, "The Obama Portraits Have Boosted Attendance to the National Portrait Gallery by More Than 300 Percent," *Artnet*, February 20, 2018. https://news.artnet.com/exhibitions/national-portrait-gallery-obamas-1228535.

Samuel Morse's portrait: "James Monroe," https://www.whitehousehistory.org/photos/james-monroe.

in 1954, a government employee: "5c James Monroe Single," https://arago.si.edu/category_2028966.html.

Monroe joins his former neighbor: Harlow Giles Unger, *The Last Founding Father* (Philadelphia: Da Capo Press, 2009).

19   **one of only a few**: Ibid. The other two presidents wounded in combat were Rutherford B. Hayes and George H. W. Bush.

he was the last president to wear breeches: Ronald P. Formisano, "James Monroe," in *The American Presidency*, ed. Alan Brinkley and Davis Dyer (Boston: Houghton Mifflin, 2004), 61.

his body was moved to Richmond: United States National Park Service, *The Presidents: From the Inauguration of George Washington to the Inauguration of Jimmy Carter, Historic Places Commemorating the Chief Executives of the United States,* 2nd ed. Ed. Robert Ferris. Washington, DC: U.S. Government Printing Office, 1977. https://www.nps.gov/parkhistory/online_books/presidents/site62.htm.

the first photo of a president: Megan Garber, "The Oldest Known Photographs of a U.S. President," *The Atlantic*, February 5, 2013.

the oldest recording is of Benjamin Harrison: "U.S. Presidential Audio Recordings, https://lib.msu.edu/vvl/presidents/harrison/.

not until almost the twentieth century do we know: Jordan Hillman, "Grover the Good," https://npg.si.edu/blog/grover-good-grover-cleveland%E2%80%99s-birthday.

20   **another forty-five years**: Erik Barnouw, *Tube of Plenty: The Evolution of American Television,* 2nd ed. (New York: Oxford University Press, 1990).

the first president to be photographed by a digital camera: Laura Jane Dziuban, "President Obama's official portrait: the first ever taken with a digital camera," *Engadget*, January 14, 2009.

the first president born in a hospital: "Jimmy Carter National Historic Site," https://www.nps.gov/nr/travel/presidents/jimmy_carter_nhs.html.

the light is wrong: "Crossing the Delaware in Art," https://www.mountvernon.org/george-washington/artwork/crossing-the-delaware-in-art/.

21   **The first photograph of a president**: The first five presidents all died before photographic technology had developed short-enough exposure times to make a portrait possible.

John Quincy Adams weeps: John Quincy Adams, *Memoirs of John Quincy Adams* (Philadelphia: J. B. Lippincott & Co, 1876), 400-401.

he spans the opening chapters of America: Adams was born in 1767 and died in 1848, having spent almost the entirety of his life in service to the United States.

his father, the second president: The Massachusetts Historical Society is the home of the Adams Family Papers, including 1,159 letters sent between John and Abigail Adams. "About the Correspondence Between John and Abigail Adams," https://www.masshist.org/digitaladams/archive/letter/.

Henry Adams: Henry Adams, *The Education of Henry Adams: An Autobiography* (Boston: Houghton Mifflin, 1918).

22   **He went everywhere**: "Biographies of the Secretaries of State: John Quincy Adams (1767-1848)," https://history.state.gov/departmenthistory/people/adams-john-quincy.

The Smithsonian exists because James Smithson: It's not a direct line. Essentially, James Smithson left all his money to his nephew, with the stipulation that if the nephew died childless, the money would go to "an Establishment for the increase and diffusion of knowledge among men" in the United States. When the nephew died without an heir, and after a few years of legal machinations on both sides of the Atlantic, Richard Rush, son of Declaration signer Benjamin Rush, brought the bequest back to the U.S. in the form of gold sovereign coins. As they were British money, the United States then melted the coins and reminted them as $10 gold coins in 1838. Meanwhile (it's really not a direct line at all), Treasury Secretary Levi Woodbury had decided the best investment for the money would be bonds issued by the new states of Michigan and Arkansas. Both states promptly defaulted, and the new coins went to pay off that loss, thereby losing Smithson's bequest forever—had Congressman John Quincy Adams not stepped in and forced the Congress to vote for full replacement of the money. For more detail, see Edwards Park, "How James Smithson's Money Built the Smithsonian," *Smithsonian Magazine*, May 1996.

The Smithsonian also exists because John Quincy Adams: Ibid.

When the Congress instituted a gag rule: Adams fighting the gag rule is an impressive manipulation of the system. If Adams couldn't introduce petitions against slavery, then he could introduce petitions in favor of it and use his position as chair to hold the floor to speak against them. His threat to his colleagues—kick me out, and my people will send me back, and what's more, this time they'll be angry—was enough to keep them from censuring him. "Historical Highlights: A Motion to Censure Representative John Quincy Adams of Massachusetts," https://history.house.gov/HistoricalHighlight/Detail/35497.

23   **painted in 1938 by Hale Woodruff**: *Rising Up: Hale Woodruff's Murals at Talladega College* (Washington, D.C.: Smithsonian National Museum of African American History and Culture, 2014).

Adams spoke for four hours: Chandra M. Manning, "John Quincy Adams (1767-1848)," in *Slavery in the United States: A Social, Political, and Historical Encyclopedia*, ed. Junius P. Rodriguez. Vol. 1 (Santa Barbara: ABC-CLIO, 2007).

24   **the first president to ride a train**: National Constitution Center, "Presidents and Trains: Tools of Power and Symbolism," https://constitution-center.org/blog/presidents-and-trains-tools-of-power-and-symbolism.

25   **because he set in motion**: Library of Congress, "Indian Removal Act: Primary Documents in American History," https://guides.loc.gov/indian-removal-act

like Whitman: Walt Whitman, "Song of Myself," *Leaves of Grass* (Philadelphia: Rees Welsh and Co, 1882).

26   **from a placemat**: Tom's Tavern, Boulder, Colorado, closed in 2009, but it was a regular stop on all Rafferty family vacations to Colorado during my childhood.

I live in a state where people argue: "Dan Snyder defends 'Redskins,'" *ESPN*, August 5, 2014. https://www.espn.com/nfl/story/_/id/11313245/daniel-snyder-redskins-term-honor-respect.

a stone-cold killer: Theo Emery, "Killed in a Duel, Then Lost in the Earth," *New York Times*, December 17, 2007, A27.

tiny waist: Smithsonian National Museum of American History, "Andrew Jackson's Uniform Coat with Epaulets," https://americanhistory.si.edu/collections/search/object/nmah_445642.

he most honors my style: Walt Whitman, "Song of Myself."

28   **There is a story about Christmas 1835**: Jon Meacham, *American Lion: Andrew Jackson in the White House* (New York: Random House, 2008).

thanks to Andrew Jackson's endorsement: Jackson probably could have won a third term, but the precedent set by Washington's two terms was so powerful that he instead retired, supporting Van Buren as the candidate. Van Buren was the last man to be elected president directly from the vice presidency until George H. W. Bush.

Jackson back to Tennessee: Ibid. Jackson left the White House three days after Van Buren's inauguration.

29 **All these things compound**: Donald B. Cole, *Martin Van Buren and the American Political System* (Princeton: Princeton University Press, 1984).

 the Little Magician: "Martin Van Buren," *Encyclopedia Britannica*. https://www.britannica.com/biography/Martin-Van-Buren.

 the Sly Fox: Ibid.

 this is how this term came to prominence: The early nineteenth century saw a fad in America of both comical misspellings and abbreviations. "O.K." emerged as an abbreviation of "Oll Korrect," and the Democrats jumped on its popularity for Van Buren's campaign. John Ciardi, "Martin Van Buren Was OK," *NPR on Words*, March 9, 2006. https://www.npr.org/templates/story/story.php?storyId=5170008

 Van, Van is a used-up man: Joel Sibley, "Martin Van Buren: Campaigns and Elections," https://millercenter.org/president/vanburen/campaigns-and-elections.

30 **he tries for eight**: Ibid. Eighty percent of eligible voters turned out in the 1840 election. Van Buren failed to win even his home state of New York.

 he tries again in '44: Cole, *Martin Van Buren and the American Political System*.

 he tries again in '48, a Free Soil Party man: Ibid. The short-lived Free Soil Party opposed slavery, especially in the territories, favored paying off the national debt, proposed giving land to settlers, and called for a protective tariff. They existed from 1848 to 1854, when most of them joined the new Republican Party.

 when he dies, the country is split: Van Buren died on July 24, 1862; on July 1, Lee had pushed McClellan back to the James River after the Battle of Malvern Hill, ending the Seven Days Battles.

31 **William Henry Harrison, Indian killer**: Robert M. Owens, *Mr. Jefferson's Hammer: William Henry Harrison and the Origins of American Indian Policy* (Norman: University of Oklahoma Press, 2007).

 falls sick, dies thirty-two days after inauguration: "William Henry Harrison," https://www.whitehouse.gov/about-the-white-house/presidents/william-henry-harrison/.

 no such thing as a mother of all bombs: Helene Cooper and Mujib Mashal, "U.S. Drops 'Mother of All Bombs' on ISIS Caves in Afghanistan." *New York Times*, April 13, 2017. The bomb is officially named the GBU-43/B Massive Ordinance Air Blast.

 a smoothbore musket is accurate to about a hundred yards: Justin Stanage, "The Rifle-Musket vs. the Smoothbore Musket, a Comparison of the Effectiveness of the Two Types of Weapons Primarily at Short Ranges." Student paper, Indiana University. https://scholarworks.iu.edu/journals/index.php/iusburj/article/view/19841/25918.

a hard cider jug shaped like a log cabin: Heckler Auctions, "The Log Cabin and Hard Cider Campaign," https://www.hecklerauction.com/news/120.html.

fifteen dollars: "Visiting Berkeley Plantation," http://www.berkeleyplantation.com/visit.html.

he'll vote to dissolve the Union: John G. Deal, "John Tyler," *Encyclopedia Virginia*, https://www.encyclopediavirginia.org/Tyler_John_1790-1862.

in one hundred and five minutes: John McCollister, *God and the Oval Office: The Religious Faith of Our 43 Presidents* (Nashville: W Publishing Group, 2005).

33   **The view is better from the other side, but he refuses**: Edward P. Crapol, *John Tyler: The Accidental President* (Chapel Hill: University of North Carolina Press, 2006).

Horseshoe Falls grinds down the clay of the riverbed: US Army Corps of Engineers, "Niagara River," https://www.lre.usace.army.mil/Missions/Great-Lakes-Information/Outflows/Discharge-Measurements/Niagara-River/. Controls on the river have slowed the rate of erosion over the years.

The Congress does not take control of the Executive branch: The Constitution only says that "In case of the removal of the President from office, or of his death, resignation, or inability to discharge the powers and duties of the said office, the same shall devolve on the Vice President, and the Congress may by law provide for the case of removal, death, resignation or inability, both of the President and Vice President, declaring what officer shall then act as President, and such officer shall act accordingly, until the disability be removed, or a President shall be elected." When Harrison died, no one was quite sure if Tyler became president or just assumed the powers of the presidency, or if he was supposed to finish Harrison's term or call for new elections. Congress, the most powerful branch of the government at the time, could easily have dictated the terms of things, but Tyler's assumption of the presidency set the precedent, which was officially codified into the Constitution by the 25th Amendment.

The Whigs leave him behind: Crapol, *John Tyler.*

34   **The visit to Niagara is a ritual**: Don Glynn, "Niagara's a Popular Stop with Presidents," *Niagara Gazette*, May 13, 2010.

he chairs the Virginia Peace Convention: Samuel Eliot Morison, "The Peace Convention of 1861," *Proceedings of the Massachusetts Historical Society*, Vol. 73, (1961): 58-80.

buried in a foreign land: I am taking poetic license here; no other country's government ever officially recognized the Confederate States of America as an independent country.

35   **"In performing for the first time"**: Miller Center, "December 2, 1845: First Annual Message." https://millercenter.org/the-presidency/presidential-speeches/december-2-1845-first-annual-message.

the incursion of foreign troops upon American soil: The war began over a border dispute in Texas. Then-Congressman Abraham Lincoln questioned Polk's claim that Mexico had invaded, asking "whether the particular spot of soil on which the blood of our citizens was shed was, or was not, our own soil." "Lincoln's Spot Resolution," https://history.house.gov/Records-and-Research/Listing/lfp_037/.

not of the American character: Miller Center, "December 2, 1845: First Annual Message."

Ulysses S. Grant and Robert E. Lee serving in the same army: "Before the War," *Lee and Grant*. (Richmond: Virginia Museum of History and Culture, 2008).

the Halls of Montezuma: the opening line of the Marine Corps hymn is in reference to their storming of Chapultepec Castle in Mexico City during the Mexican-American War. The castle was built by the Spanish and not the Aztecs.

one thousand, seven hundred and thirty-three men killed: Micheal Clodfelter, *Warfare and Armed Conflicts: A Statistical Encyclopedia of Casualty and Other Figures, 1492-2015*, 4th ed. (Jefferson, NC: McFarland and Company, 2017).

36   a written document: "List of In-Person Annual Message and State of the Union Addresses," https://history.house.gov/Institution/SOTU/List/.

"As the wisdom, strength, and beneficence": "December 8, 1846: Second Annual Message to Congress," https://millercenter.org/the-presidency/presidential-speeches/december-8-1846-second-annual-message-congress.

who owns more than fifty men at his death: Ted Ownby, "James K. Polk," *Mississippi Encyclopedia,* https://mississippiencyclopedia.org/entries/james-k-polk/.

eight-percent cash profit: William Dusinberre, *Slavemaster President: The Double Career of James Polk* (New York: Oxford University Press, 2003).

a meeting between past and future: Lincoln served a single term (1847-49) in Congress as a Whig, where he met John Quincy Adams, who had served as ambassador to the Netherlands in the Washington administration. Amanda A. Mathews, "When Adams Met Lincoln," *The Beehive* (Boston: Massachusetts Historical Society, December 12, 2012).

37   **"It has ever been our cherished policy"**: "December 7, 1847: Third Annual Message." https://millercenter.org/the-presidency/presidential-speeches/december-7-1847-third-annual-message.

dead three months after leaving office: Walter R. Borneman, *Polk: The Man Who Transformed the Presidency and America* (New York: Random House, 2009).

"It may, indeed, be truly said": "December 5, 1848: Fourth Annual Message to Congress." https://millercenter.org/the-presidency/presidential-speeches/december-5-1848-fourth-annual-message-congress.

38   **seven presidents have been born in log cabins**: Jackson, Taylor, Fillmore, Buchanan, Lincoln, Grant, and Garfield. Of the forty-five presidents, more entered this world in log cabins than did in hospitals.

a log cabin that served as an outbuilding: "Historic Sites: Montebello, Birthplace of President Zachary Taylor," https://www.virginia.org/listings/HistoricSites/MontebelloBirthplaceofPresidentZacharyTaylor/.

likely from cholera: Michael Holt, "Zachary Taylor: Death of the President," https://millercenter.org/president/taylor/death-of-the-president.

Antaeus, the giant of Greek mythology: The story of Antaeus gaining his strength from the Earth is told in Book IX of Ovid's *Metamorphoses*.

40   **Zachary Taylor was followed by rumors of poisoning**: Michael Marriott, "Zachary Taylor's Remains Are Removed for Tests," *New York Times*, June 18, 1991, A10.

41   **"The Union Is Saved!"**: James McPherson, *Battle Cry of Freedom: The Civil War Era* (New York, Oxford University Press, 1988).

it's his name on the letter: "Letters from U.S. President Millard Fillmore and U.S. Navy Commodore Matthew C. Perry to the Emperor of Japan (1852-1853)," http://afe.easia.columbia.edu/ps/japan/fillmore_perry_letters.pdf. The idea that the emperor was a god continued until Emperor Hirohito issued the Humanity Declaration in the wake of the Japanese surrender in World War II, effectively separating church and state in Japan (and in himself).

Perry turns away: "The United States and the Opening to Japan, 1853," https://2001-2009.state.gov/r/pa/ho/time/dwe/86550.htm.

42   **He had the biggest library**: Douglas P. McElrath, review of *The First White House Library: A History and Annotated Catalogue*, by Catherine M. Parisian, *The Library Quarterly: Information, Community, Policy*, vol. 81, no. 3, 2011.

the painter Kano Kazunobu begins: *Masters of Mercy: Buddha's Amazing Disciples*, (Washington, DC: Arthur M. Sackler Gallery, 2012).

the disciples . . . are capable of amazing feats: Ibid.

the hungry ghosts are the reincarnations: Erik Davis, *Deathpower: Buddhism's Ritual Imagination in Cambodia* (New York: Columbia University Press, 2015).

Kazunobu works on these paintings: *Masters of Mercy*.

43 **In his final notable act**: The American Party, better known as the Know Nothing Party existed from 1851-1858, running on an anti-immigrant, nativist, and anti-Catholic platform. The name is derived from its members' refusal to speak about the secret society from which the party evolved. "The Know Nothing Party," https://exhibits.library.villanova.edu/chaos-in-the-streets-the-philadelphia-riots-of-1844/know-nothings.

They are installed in the temple: *Masters of Mercy*.

in 2012 they travel: Ibid.

44 **who has recently resigned his senate seat**: Roy Franklin Nichols, *Franklin Pierce: Young Hickory of the Granite Hills* (Philadelphia: University of Pennsylvania Press, 1958).

we have had the railways for only fifteen years: The Baltimore and Ohio Railroad began operations in 1827. Library of Congress, "First U.S. Railway Chartered to Transport Freight and Passengers," http://www.americaslibrary.gov/jb/nation/jb_nation_train_1.html.

who has recently returned from the conquest: Nichols, *Franklin Pierce*.

45 **received a hero's welcome in Concord**: Ibid.

who recently suffered trauma in a train wreck: Ibid.

patient's wife stays to her own rooms: Ibid.

Soldier's heart. Battle fatigue: Matthew J. Friedman, "History of PTSD in Veterans: Civil War to DSM-5," U.S. Department of Veterans Affairs, https://www.ptsd.va.gov/understand/what/history_ptsd.asp.

46 **The man and the hour have met**: This was said by William Yancey, a Confederate senator, in reference to Jefferson Davis's becoming the president of the C.S.A.

the patient caused Kansas to bleed: American Battlefield Trust, "Bleeding Kansas," https://www.battlefields.org/learn/articles/bleeding-kansas.

47 ***A house is a machine for living in***: Le Corbusier, *Towards an Architecture* (Los Angeles: Getty Research Institute, 2007).

one half of the house: Philip Shriver Klein, *The Story of Wheatland* (Lancaster: Junior League of Lancaster, 1936).

48 **the subject of whispers and rumors**: Thomas Balcerski, "The 175-Year History of Speculating about President James Buchanan's Bachelorhood," *Smithsonian Magazine*, August 27, 2019.

he could hear the cannon fire: Lancaster is about fifty-five miles from Gettysburg, as the crow flies.

49   **Edward Everett quotes Pericles**: Edward Everett, "Gettysburg Address," *Voices of Democracy,* https://voicesofdemocracy.umd.edu/everett-gettysburg-address-speech-text/.

over the wires, just as his orders: David Homer Bates, *Lincoln in the Telegraph Office: Recollections of the United States Military Telegraph Corps During the Civil War.* (Lincoln, NE: Bison Books, 1995).

his three hundred thousand more: The poet James Sloan Gibbons published a poem, "We Are Coming, Father Abra'am," in the July 16, 1862, issue of the *Saturday Evening Post,* which was later set to music by several different composers. The song references Lincoln's call for three hundred thousand volunteers to join the armed forces that month.

50   **(a photographer captures this)**: Matthew Brady was the photographer, but it wasn't until 1952 that Josephine Cobb, chief of the Still Photo section of the National Archives, discovered the Brady had captured Lincoln on the platform at Gettysburg. Rob Crotty, "Rare Photo of Lincoln at Gettysburg," *Pieces of History* (Washington, DC: National Archives, November 19, 2010).

51   **his wife over his shoulder guiding him**: Elizabeth Varon, "Andrew Johnson: Life Before the Presidency," https://millercenter.org/president/johnson/life-before-the-presidency.

Years from now, when others could do it for him: "Andrew Johnson," *Encyclopedia Britannica,* https://www.britannica.com/biography/Andrew-Johnson.

52   **He buys a slave, his constitutional right**: Ibid.

He is likely drunk when he takes the oath: Ibid.

The North sees him giving away the victory: William S. McFeely, *Grant* (New York: W. W. Norton & Company, 2002).

53   **the Congress impeaches him**: "The Impeachment of Andrew Johnson (1868) President of the United States," https://www.senate.gov/artandhistory/history/common/briefing/Impeachment_Johnson.htm.

stitched into an American flag: National Park Service, "Andrew Johnson National Historic Site," https://www.nps.gov/nr/travel/presidents/andrew_johnson_nhs.html.

55   **a shell lands**: James F. Dunnigan and Daniel Masterson, *The Way of the Warrior: Business Tactics and Techniques from History's Twelve Greatest Generals* (New York: St. Martin's Publishing, 2014).

the many thousands: Gregory Mertz, "Battle of the Wilderness," *Encyclopedia Virginia,* https://www.encyclopediavirginia.org/Battle_of_the_Wilderness.

6.8 meters per second, per second: Credit goes to Mr. Perry, my high school physics teacher, for this and a million other things that I think about all the time.

56 **when the firefight set the forest alight**: Mertz, "Battle of the Wilderness."

says an officer: Gordon C. Rhea, *In the Footsteps of Grant and Lee: The Wilderness Through Cold Harbor* (Baton Rouge: Louisiana State University Press, 2007).

57 **Grant couldn't stand the sight of blood**: Ron Chernow, *Grant* (New York: Penguin Press, 2017).

the northern papers: Edward H. Bonekemper II, "The Butcher's Bill," https://www.historynet.com/the-butchers-bill.htm.

Grant turned right: James C. Bradford, ed. *Oxford Atlas of American Military History* (New York: Oxford University Press, 2003).

Grant and the Union Army marched south: Ibid.

58 **loses most of the South**: Jean Edward Smith, *Grant* (New York: Simon and Schuster, 2002).

sick with cancer, rushing to save his family. Ibid.

of the Wilderness, he wrote: Ulysses S. Grant, *Memoirs and Selected Letters* (New York: Library of America, 1990).

59 **An autopsy is the act of seeing with one's own eyes**: "autopsy, n." *OED Online* (New York: Oxford University Press, March 2020), www.oed.com/view/Entry/13519.

weigh their organs like Anubis in the underworld: Philip Wilkinson, *Myths and Legends: An Illustrated Guide to Their Origins and Meanings* (London: DK Press, 2009).

Little Fanny Hayes has two dollhouses: "Our Permanent Collections," https://www.rbhayes.org/estate/core-exhibits/.

He was wounded five times during the war: Ari Hoogenboom, *Rutherford B. Hayes: Warrior and President.* (Lawrence: University Press of Kansas, 1995).

He preferred "General Hayes" to "Mister President": Learned on a tour of Spiegel Grove, 2012.

Large and mahogany: Henry L. Fry, Large Mahogany Sideboard, 1880. Rutherford B. Hayes Library. Postcard.

60 **the army chases the Nez Perce to Bear Paw**: "Battle of Bear Paw," *Missoulian,* 6 September 2017.

Sardis Birchard built the home: "Spiegel Grove: The Hayes Estate," https://www.rbhayes.org/estate/spiegel-grove/.

believe, as Sardis Birchard did, that this place might be from the fairy tales: Ibid.

the deal Hayes and the Republicans cut: Hoogenboom, *Rutherford B. Hayes.*

it took 132 years: Blanche K. Bruce represented Mississippi from 1875 to 1881. Tim Scott of South Carolina was appointed to the Senate in 2013.

61 **the Easter Egg Roll on the White House lawn:** White House Historical Association, "Easter Egg Roll: President Hayes Saves the Day," https://www.whitehousehistory.org/easter-egg-roll-president-hayes.

the country's flags went to half-staff: Nancy Hendricks, *America's First Ladies: A Historical Encyclopedia and Primary Document Collection of the Remarkable Women of the White House* (Santa Barbara: ABC-CLIO, 2015).

for less than four dollars: In 2012, when I visited Spiegel Grove and purchased the postcard collection, the United States Postal Service charged 32 cents for a postcard stamp.

63 **A train station once stood here:** Jason Daley, "Why Doesn't Garfield Assassination Site on the National Mall Have a Marker?" *Smithsonian Magazine,* January 25, 2018.

a gun he thought would look good in a museum: Ibid.

lingers two and a half months: Ibid.

the train station lasts longer: Ibid.

Andrew Mellon . . . builds the National Gallery of Art: "Gallery History," https://www.nga.gov/about/creating-the-museum.html.

64 **Grew up poor:** Justus Doenecke, "James A. Garfield: Life in Brief," https://millercenter.org/president/garfield/life-in-brief.

He later lamented the lack of a father figure: Allen Peskin, *Garfield: A Biography* (Kent, OH: Kent State University Press, 1978).

Born again at eighteen: Justus Donecke, "James A. Garfield: Life Before the Presidency," https://millercenter.org/president/garfield/life-before-the-presidency.

whatever lets him pursue his education: Ibid.

He's in the war: Ibid.

sees the war as a holy crusade against slavery: Ibid.

Horatio Alger wrote his campaign biography: Horatio Alger, *From Canal Boy to President, or the Boyhood and Manhood of James A. Garfield* (New York: American Publishers Corporation, 1881).

65   **He believes in waving the bloody flag**: James C. Humes, *My Fellow Americans: Presidential Addresses that Shaped History* (Santa Barbara: Praeger, 1992).

He's a little corrupt: Robert C. Kennedy, "'Every Public Question With An Eye Only To The Public Good,'" *On This Day. New York Times,* https://archive.nytimes.com/www.nytimes.com/learning/general/onthisday/harp/0315.html.

He oversees the 1876 recount in Louisiana: Peskin, *Garfield.*

the Democrats still make rumbles about tampering: Ibid.

he was left-handed: Rumors abound that Garfield, who spoke several languages, was not only ambidextrous, but could simultaneously write Greek with one hand and Latin with the other.

67   **they say he was born in Canada**: Arthur Milnes, "A Canadian U.S. President? It Wouldn't Be the First Time," *Times Union* (Albany, NY), April 6, 2015.

they said that Frémont was a Catholic: Andrew F. Rolle, *John Charles Frémont: Character As Destiny* (Norman, OK: University of Oklahoma Press, 1991).

they said that Jefferson had mixed blood: Albert Jay Nock, *Jefferson* (Auburn, AL: Ludwig von Mises Institute, 2007).

they said that Jackson was a bigamist: Patricia Brady, *A Being So Gentle: The Frontier Love Story of Rachel and Andrew Jackson* (New York: St. Martin's Press, 2011).

he never knew the smell of gunpowder: Quotation from an anti-Arthur pamphlet by A. P. Hinman, *How a British Subject Became President of the United States* (New York: 1884).

I am a stalwart of the Stalwarts: Jay Bellamy, "A Stalwart of Stalwarts: Garfield's Assassin Sees Deed as Special Duty," *Prologue*, Vol. 48, No. 3, Fall 2016.

68   **they find a New York Supreme Court justice**: "The Swearing In of Chester A. Arthur: September 20, 1881," Joint Congressional Committee on Inaugural Ceremonies, https://www.inaugural.senate.gov/about/past-inaugural-ceremonies/swearing-in-of-vice-president-chester-arthur-after-the-assassination-of-president-james-garfield/.

They say they could have saved him: Candice Millard, *Destiny of the Republic: A Tale of Madness, Medicine, and the Murder of a Presiden.* (New York: Doubleday, 2011).

He does not give patronage jobs to cronies: National Archives, "Pendleton Act (1883)." *Our Documents.* https://www.ourdocuments.gov/doc.php?flash=false&doc=48.

a breach of the national faith: "The Veto," *Harper's Weekly*, April 15, 1882.

not for the common defense: "Message," *State Papers, Etc., Etc., Etc., of Chester A. Arthur, President of the United State*s (Washington, D.C.: Government Printing Office, 1885).

he signs a revision of the bill: National Archives, "Chinese Exclusion Act (1882)," *Our Documents,* https://www.ourdocuments.gov/doc.php?flash=false&doc=47.

in front of the Indian market: Kaluystan's, of which Alana N. on Yelp says "I'm like a kid in a candy store in here! It's a foodie wonderland. Any ingredient you think you're going to have trouble finding, you can find it here."

70   **just four years**: H. Paul Jeffers, *An Honest President: The Life and Presidencies of Grover Cleveland* (New York: William Morrow, 2000).

civilize the Indian by breaking their common land: National Archives, "Dawes Act (1887)," *Our Documents,* https://www.ourdocuments.gov/doc.php?flash=false&doc=50.

71   **the war you paid another man to fight**: Henry F. Graff, "Grover Cleveland: Life Before the Presidency," https://millercenter.org/president/cleveland/life-before-the-presidency.

veto bills to grant more pensions: Grover Cleveland, "February 11, 1887: Veto of Military Pension Legislation," https://millercenter.org/the-presidency/presidential-speeches/february-11-1887-veto-military-pension-legislation.

return the South's battle flags: Henry F. Graff, "Grover Cleveland: Impact and Legacy," https://millercenter.org/president/cleveland/impact-and-legacy.

you'll marry in the White House: Cleveland is the only president to get married in the White House itself (Tyler and Wilson both married while in office, but not in the White House), marrying twenty-one-year-old Frances Folsom on June 2, 1886.

you still win the popular vote: Richard Pallardy, "United States Presidential Election of 1888," *Encyclopedia Britannica.* https://www.britannica.com/event/United-States-presidential-election-of-1888.

your wife tells the staff: S. J. Ackerman, "The First Celebrity First Lady: Frances Cleveland," *Washington Post Magazine*, June 27, 2014.

73   **the Edison cylinder recording the speech**: Vincent Voice Library, Michigan State University, "U.S. Presidential Audio Recordings," https://lib.msu.edu/vvl/presidents/harrison/.

find him and his presidential grandfather: *World Book Encyclopedia*, Vol. 9, 2018.

Harrison knew volunteers: Charles Calhoun, *Benjamin Harrison* (New York: Macmillan, 2005).

families sweeping a tombstone on Memorial Day: Daniel Bellware and Richard Gardines, *The Genesis of the Memorial Day Holiday in America* (Columbus: Columbus State University Press, 2014).

click through the edit history: available at https://en.wikipedia.org/w/index.php?title=Benjamin_Harrison&action=history.

a president invested in technology: Harrison had electricity installed at the White House, but both he and his wife, Caroline, did not touch the switches, out of fear. United States Department of Energy, "The History of Electricity at the White House," October 14, 2015, https://www.energy.gov/articles/history-electricity-white-house.

75   **she of candy-bar fame**: Pernell Watson, "Candy Bar Named for Kid . . . Maybe," *Daily Press* (Newport News, VA), February 26, 2003.

this time the Senate fights you: H. Paul Jeffers, *An Honest President: The Life and Presidencies of Grover Cleveland* (New York: William Morrow, 2000).

a railroad strike you'll try to break: Grover Cleveland, "July 8, 1894: Proclamation Regarding Railroad Strike," https://millercenter.org/the-presidency/presidential-speeches/july-8-1894-proclamation-regarding-railroad-strike.

76   **an army of men will march on Washington**: Carlos A. Schwantes, *Coxey's Army: An American Odyssey* (Lincoln: University of Nebraska Press, 1985).

the businessmen in Hawaii who overthrow the queen: James L. Haley, *Captive Paradise: A History of Hawaii.* (New York: St. Martin's Press, 2014).

a secret surgery on board the presidential yacht: The tumor removed is on view at the Mütter Museum in Philadelphia, Pennsylvania.

run by silverites, nominating another man: Jeffers, *An Honest President.*

77   **"I have tried so hard to do right"**: Ibid.

78   **The organist starts to play**: Scott Miller, *The President and the Assassin: McKinley, Terror, and Empire at the Dawn of the American Century* (New York: Random House, 2011).

his right hand wrapped in a handkerchief: "McKinley Is Shot Down," *Chicago Eagle*, Vol. 24, no. 623, September 14, 1901.

mourners would drape the pictures: Marilyn A. Mendoza, "Death and Mourning Practices in the Victorian Age," *Psychology Today*, December 8, 2018.

79   **an x-ray machine . . . is on display**: Miller, *The President and the Assassin.*

The Secret Service has only begun protecting the president: United States Secret Service, "USSS History," https://www.secretservice.gov/about/history/events/.

Cortelyou asks the president not to attend: H. Wayne Morgan, *William McKinley and His America* (Kent: Kent State University Press, 1998).

a 1900 campaign poster shows McKinley: Larry Margasak, "Silver vs. Gold: William Steinway's Wedge Issue of the 1896 Election," *O Say Can You See: Stories from the Museum* (Washington, DC: National Museum of American History, October 29, 2014), https://americanhistory.si.edu/blog/silver-vs-gold-william-steinways-wedge-issue-1896-election.

McKinley is re-elected by almost a million more votes: Richard Pallardy, "United States Presidential Election of 1900," *Encyclopedia Britannica,* https://www.britannica.com/event/United-States-presidential-election-of-1900.

a victim of the Curse of Tecumseh: Robert Pohl, *Urban Legends and Historic Lore of Washington, DC* (Charleston, SC: The History Press, 2013).

80   **the word *assassin* has its origin**: "assassin, n." *OED Online* (New York: Oxford University Press, March 2020), www.oed.com/view/Entry/11728.

Leon Czolgosz . . . was electrocuted: Amy Tikkanen, "Leon Czolgosz: American Assassin," *Encyclopedia Britannica.* https://www.britannica.com/biography/Leon-Czolgosz.

Doctors operated on him: H. Wayne Morgan, *William McKinley and His America* (Kent: Kent State University Press, 1998).

After the surgery: Ibid.

was an anarchist: Michael Newton, *Age of Assassins: A History of Conspiracy and Political Violence, 1865-1901* (New York: Faber & Faber, 2012).

81   **he had driven rations**: National Park Service, "Monument to William McKinley," https://www.nps.gov/anti/learn/historyculture/mnt-mckinley.htm.

a gun bought for $4.50: Susan Berfield, "The Consequential Last Act of Leon Czolgosz," *Lapham's Quarterly*, May 5, 2020,https://www.laphamsquarterly.org/roundtable/consequential-last-act-leon-czolgosz.

Thomas Edison made a film: Thomas Edison, "Execution of Czolgosz, with Panorama of Auburn Prison," Library of Congress. https://www.loc.gov/item/00694362.

McKinley deteriorated on the seventh day: Morgan, *William McKinley and His America.*

82   **The Confederate army band played the song**: Dave and Sharon Oester, *Ghosts of Gettysburg: Walking on Hallowed Ground* (New York: iUniverse, 2007).

Garfield's funeral: Louis L. Piccone, *The President Is Dead! The Extraordinary Stories of Presidential Deaths, Final Days, Burials, and Beyond* (New York: Skyhorse Books, 2016).

Ford's funeral: Joint Committee on Print, "Memorial Services in the Congress of the United States and Tributes in Eulogy of Gerald R. Ford, Late a President of the United States." 2007.

They'll play it on the *Titanic*: Richard Parton Howells, *The Myth of the Titanic*, (New York: Palgrave Macmillan, 1999).

the song is sung to the tune of "Bethany" "Nearer My God to Thee: The History and Lyrics," The Tabernacle Choir Blog, September 30, 2014. https://www.thetabernaclechoir.org/articles/nearer-my-god-to-thee-history-and-lyrics.html.

a little after two o'clock that night: "The President Passes Away," *Washington Times,* September 14, 1901.

83   **they call him** *teedie* **as a boy**: National Park Service, "History and Culture," https://www.nps.gov/thrb/learn/historyculture/index.htm.

j p wood's *natural history*: Learned on a tour of the Theodore Roosevelt Birthplace, May 2015.

his father is the one who can best convince his lungs: Kathleen Dalton, *Theodore Roosevelt: A Strenuous Life* (New York: Vintage, 2004).

selfishness or cruelty, idleness, cowardice, or untruthfulness: Quoted in National Park Service, "Theodore Roosevelt, Sr." https://www.nps.gov/thrb/learn/historyculture/theodorerooseveltsr.htm.

who paid another man to take his place: Ibid.

inviting booker t washington to dinner: Dalton, *Theodore Roosevelt.*

84   **the safari to africa after leaving office**: Ibid.

the least powerful position in america: John Nance Garner, one of FDR's vice presidents, famously referred to the position as "not worth a bucket of warm spit" and "the spare tire on the automobile of government." US Senate, "John Nance Garner," https://www.senate.gov/artandhistory/art/artifact/Painting_31_00007.htm.

means well but he means feebly: Theodore Roosevelt, "Address of Hon. Theodore Roosevelt, Delivered at Boston," April 27, 1912, https://archive.org/stream/addressofhonthe00roos/addressofhonthe00roos_djvu.txt.

the river of doubt: Candice Millard, *The River of Doubt: Theodore Roosevelt's Darkest Journey*. (New York: Doubleday, 2005).

shot down over germany: Dalton, *Theodore Roosevelt*.

85   ***the old lion is dead***: Ibid.

86   **He did get stuck in the White House bathtub**: Or maybe not? The story seems to originate from Ike Hoover's 1934 memoir *Forty-Two Years in the White House*, but contemporary historians point out that there are no supporting documentations of this. It seems fitting that the most famous thing about William H. Taft is a story that might not be true.

He wrestled too: Bob Dellinger, "Wrestling in the USA." National Wrestling Hall of Fame, https://nwhof.org/stillwater/resources-library/history/wrestling-in-the-usa/.

87   **asks Taft to govern the new American territory**: Judith Icke Anderson, *William Howard Taft: An Intimate History*. (New York: Norton, 1981).

had opposed annexation: Ibid.

his commitment to his decision is such: Ibid.

88   **his friend Roosevelt turns on him**: Dalton, *Theodore Roosevelt*.

starting in 1948, surveys…rank him near the middle: Gary M. Maranell, "The Evaluation of Presidents: An Extension of the Schlesinger Polls" *Journal of American History*, Vol. 57, No. 1 (June 1970). A 2017 ranking done by 170 members of the American Political Science Association ranked Taft at twenty-second.

"why a man who is so good as chief justice": Melvin Urofsky, *Louis D Brandeis: A Life*. (New York: Schocken, 2009).

an ambitious wife: "Helen Taft." https://millercenter.org/president/taft/essays/taft-1909-firstlady.

he convinces Congress to build the Court its own home: Architect of the Capitol, "Supreme Court Building," https://www.aoc.gov/capitol-buildings/supreme-court-building.

89   **one podium from which every case is argued**: Learned on a tour of the Supreme Court Building, June 2009.

90   **a small vessel in Woodrow Wilson's brain burst**: John Milton Cooper, Jr. *Woodrow Wilson: A Biography* (New York: Vintage, 2011).

the three pounds inside his skull: P. Hartmann, et al., "Normal Weight of the Brain in Adults in Relation to Age, Sex, Body Height, and Weight," *Pathologe*, Vol. 15, No. 3 (June 1994).

three speeches a day: "October 2, 1919: U.S. President Woodrow Wilson Suffers Massive Stroke," *This Day in History,* https://www.history.com/this-day-in-history/u-s-president-woodrow-wilson-suffers-massive-stroke.

if you are as happy in entering the White house: Jean H. Baker, *James Buchanan* (New York: Times Books, 2004).

91   **Wilson vanishes from the public eye**: Cooper, Jr. *Woodrow Wilson.*

His wife, Edith, runs things: Judith L. Weaver, "Edith Bolling Wilson as First Lady: A Study in the Power of Personality, 1919-1920," *Presidential Studies Quarterly*, Vol. 15, No. 1 (Winter 1985).

He has an elevator in the house: Learned on a tour of the Woodrow Wilson House, Spring 2012.

92   **enshrined it in the federal government**: Dick Lehr, "The Racist Legacy of Woodrow Wilson," *The Atlantic*, November 27, 2015.

now is the time for all good men: Charles Weller, *The Early History of the Typewriter* (La Porte, IN: Chase & Shepherd, 1918).

she died the day the Woodrow Wilson Bridge: Joe Burris, "His Shot at Traffic Payback," *Baltimore Sun*, August 25, 2006.

93   **from a room in Chicago's Blackstone Hotel**: The Blackstone is still open, and they advertise the "Smoke Filled Suite" as an option for visiting guests. https://www.theblackstonehotel.com/stay/suites/smoke-filled -suite.

so surprised she accidentally jabs your political manager: Harry M. Daugherty and Thomas Dixon, *The Inside Story of the Harding Tragedy,* (New York: Churchill Company, 1932).

8,000 photos of you: John A. Morello, *Selling the President, 1920: Albert D. Lasker, Advertising, and the Election of Warren G. Harding* (Santa Barbara, CA: Praeger, 2001).

they'll train speakers to go around the country. Ibid.

94   *return to normalcy*: Library of Congress, "Presidential Election of 1920," https://www.loc.gov/collections/world-war-i-and-1920-election-recordings/articles-and-essays/from-war-to-normalcy/presidential-election-of-1920/.

your feet will never touch it again: Andrew Sinclair, *The Available Man: The Life Behind the Masks of Warren Gamaliel Harding* (New York: Macmillan, 1965).

a little place called Teapot Dome: Ibid.

they meet in a green house on K Street: "'Little Green House' Loses Secretiveness: Capital's Alleged Centre of 'Deals' Under Harding Remodeled for Mere Business," *New York Times*, September 3, 1931.

I have no trouble with my enemies: Eric F. Goldman, "A Sort of Rehabilitation of Warren G. Harding," *New York Times*, March 26, 1972.

95 **in the shooting pains down the left arm**: Sinclair, *The Available Man.*

the surveys of historians rank you near the bottom: The same 2017 ranking done by 170 members of the American Political Science Association that put Taft at twenty-second ranked Harding at thirty-ninth.

96 **two women approach him**: "Calvin Coolidge," *Encyclopedia Britannica,* https://www.britannica.com/biography/Calvin-Coolidge.

in the middle of the night, a messenger arrived: Robert Sobel, *Coolidge: An American Enigma* (Washington, D.C.: Regnery, 2000).

97 **Washington was apparently very quiet**: Fisher Ames, representative from Massachusetts, said that Washington's voice was "deep, a little tremulous, and so low as to call for close attention," "George Washington's Voice," https://www.mountvernon.org/george-washington/facts/washingtons-voice/.

Lincoln's voice was high-pitched: Ronald C. White Jr., *A. Lincoln: A Biography* (New York: Random House, 2009).

the Boston police strike: Sobel, *Coolidge.*

98 **he tried to pass an anti-lynching bill**: Ibid.

Ronald Reagan hung a portrait of Coolidge: John Hendrickson, "Calvin Coolidge and Ronald Reagan," Coolidge Foundation blog, October 30, 2014, https://www.coolidgefoundation.org/blog/calvin-coolidg-and-ronald-reagan/.

99 **Three decades and a year**: Hoover was fifty-eight when he left office in 1933. David E. Hamilton, "Herbert Hoover: Life After the Presidency," https://millercenter.org/president/hoover/life-after-the-presidency.

Stanford's best and brightest: Hoover, the first president born west of the Mississippi River, was a member of Stanford's inaugural class. Stanford is now home to the Hoover Institute on War, Revolution, and Peace. https://www.hoover.org/about/herbert-hoover.

he fed Belgium during the first war: David Burner, *Herbert Hoover: A Public Life* (New York: Knopf Doubleday, 1979).

served ably as Secretary of Commerce: Ibid.

100 **in his inaugural, he pledged**: Herbert Hoover, "Inaugural Address," March 4, 1929.

the unemployment rate went from 3.2% to 8.7%: "Unemployment Under Presidencies Since Depression," *New York Times,* October 9, 1982.

a quarter of the country's working force: Otis L. Graham, Jr., *Toward a Planned Society: From Roosevelt to Nixon* (New York: Oxford University Press, 1976).

stands a clock: Author visit to Waldorf Astoria Hotel, May 2015.

he has that private entrance: Sam Roberts, "Inside the Waldorf Astoria's Presidential Suite," *New York Times*, February 12, 2015.

who took Hoover's name off that dam: US Bureau of Reclamation, "The Story of Hoover Dam," https://www.usbr.gov/lc/hooverdam/history/articles/naming.html.

he's too ill to watch: Burner, *Herbert Hoover.*

101   **Odysseus's dog recognizing him**: Homer, *The Odyssey*, Book 17, lines 290-327.

102   **They built the cemetery in the county seat**: "Carroll County," United States Works Progress Administration (Iowa) Special Reports and Narratives of Projects, MS 409, Special Collections Department, Iowa State University Library.

I know he interned American citizens: What the Department of War Did in Inyo County, California, history is a question of who's writing it, and history is a question of what gets put in the front and what gets put in the endnotes. And so here it is: eight years after the Works Progress Administration built the storm sewer system, drains and gutters, even a cemetery for the people of Carroll County, Iowa, including my grandparents, Franklin Delano Roosevelt signed Executive Order 9066, which gave the Secretary of War the power to incarcerate American citizens into camps. The military, through the power of this executive order, established camps in which these citizens of the United States could be concentrated—"concentration camps," we might call them, although we called them "relocation centers," and in 1942—the same year construction of the gas chambers at Birkenau began—the United States relocated[2] a few hundred Italian Americans, a few thousand German Americans, and over one hundred thousand Japanese Americans.

The military built ten camps[3] around the country, including one in Inyo County, California, in the town of Manzanar. The relocated Americans were from places like Los Angeles, San Francisco, and Seattle, places that didn't have the scorching heat and subzero winters that Manzanar did. Generally, the military had given these citizens a week to sell their belongings except for what they could carry. A generation lost their homes and businesses[4], their livelihoods and livings, and moved into an ersatz city. There, they did the same work that the Works Progress Administration did in Carroll County, Iowa—they dug irrigation canals and ditches, farmed what they could from the fields—and beyond, establishing a news-

---

2   John Christgau, *Enemies: World War II Alien Internment* (Lincoln, NE: Bison Books, 2009).
3   Peggy Daniels Becker, *Defining Moments: Japanese-American Internment During World War II* (Detroit: Omnigraphics, 2014).
4   Ibid.

paper, dance programs, churches, temples. When the telegrams came to the gold star mothers, they helped them grieve their sons' deaths. Their sons died fighting for a country that didn't trust them or their families.

Fifty years after the Department of War moved American citizens into its own variety of concentration camps, forty-six years after the camps were shut down, and sixteen years after President Ford finally terminated Executive Order 9066, the government established Manzanar National Historic Site[5], overseen by the National Park Service, who have built a visitor center, and who lead tours of the site upon request.

There's a mention of Executive Order 9066 in the main section of this book. I could have done more in that space, but instead I told the story of how midwestern families' lives were improved by the Roosevelt Administration and not the story of how West Coast families' lives were destroyed by it. Like the National Park Service, preserving Manzanar out in Inyo County, California, leading tours and preserving the site; like the United States government, formally apologizing and paying reparations to its wrongly imprisoned citizens, I offer this endnote as a corrective—one too small and too late, but an attempt nonetheless to right—to write—the wrong.

he tried to pack the Supreme Court: H. W. Brands, *Traitor to His Class: The Privileged Life and Radical Presidency of Franklin Delano Roosevelt* (New York: Anchor, 2009).

"Carroll County, in normal years": "Carroll County."

103   **hosted him at Hyde Park and served hot dogs**: Kat Eschner, "When Franklin Delano Roosevelt Served Hot Dogs to a King," *Smithsonian Magazine*, June 12, 2017.

on March 6, 1936, the WPA employed: "Carroll County."

could invest in air-conditioning and a remodeling: "75 Years Ago," *Coon Rapids Enterprise*, July 19, 2012.

would one day propose: Interview with Geraldine Rafferty, April 2018.

104   **he'd taught himself to walk in braces**: Brands, *Traitor to His Class*.

he designed and built his own wheelchair: Ibid.

"rolling hills appear like waves": Workers of the Writers' Program of the Works Progress Administration in the State of Iowa, *Iowa: A Guide to the Hawkeye State* (Des Moines: State Historical Society of Iowa, 1938).

---

5   United States Congress, "An Act to Establish the Manzanar National Historic Site in the State of California, and for Other Purposes," Public Law 102-248, March 3, 1992, https://uscode.house.gov/statutes/pl/102/248.pdf.

106   **sealed and can never be opened again:** I first encountered the idea of
        the infinity room in Kristen Iversen's incredible and incredibly terrifying
        Full Body Burden: Growing Up in the Nuclear Shadow of Rocky Flats (New York:
        Crown, 2012).

        26 million dead: Ishaan Tharoor, "Don't Forget How the Soviet Union
        Saved the World from Hitler" *Washington Post*, May 8, 2015.

        plans made for the American invasion of Japan: D. M. Giangreco, *Hell
        to Pay: Operation DOWNFALL and the Invasion of Japan, 1945-1947* (Annap-
        olis, MD: Naval Institute Press, 2010).

        young lieutenant Truman: David McCullough, *Truman* (New York: Si-
        mon and Schuster, 1992).

        knows their telltale scents: Center for Disease Control and Prevention,
        "Facts About Phosgene," https://emergency.cdc.gov/agent/phosgene/ba-
        sics/facts.asp; "Facts About Sulfur Mustard." https://emergency.cdc.gov/
        agent/sulfurmustard/basics/facts.asp.

107   **a young boy is fitted for his first pair of eyeglasses:** McCullough, *Truman.*

        some people ask him: Laura Hein and Mark Selden, eds., *Living with the
        Bombs: American and Japanese Cultural Conflicts in the Nuclear Age* (Armonk,
        NY: M. E. Sharpe, 1997).

        half a million Purple Hearts: Kathryn Moore and D.M. Giangreco,
        "Half a Million Purple Hearts," *American Heritage*, Vol. 51, Issue 8, De-
        cember 2000.

108   **Dorothy looks at the farmhands:** *The Wizard of Oz*, directed by Victor
        Fleming, performances by Judy Garland, Ray Bolger, Jack Haley, and Burt
        Lahr. Warner Brothers, 1939.

        although he'll return: Texas Historical Commission, "Eisenhower
        Birthplace History," https://www.thc.texas.gov/historic-sites/eisenhow-
        er-birthplace/eisenhower-birthplace-history.

        the army mobilizes over terrible roads: Federal Highway Administra-
        tion, "Why President Dwight D. Eisenhower Understood We Needed the
        Interstate System," US Department of Transportation, https://www.
        fhwa.dot.gov/interstate/brainiacs/eisenhowerinterstate.cfm.

109   **so he watches, witnesses:** "The things I saw beggar description . . . the
        visual evidence and the verbal testimony of starvation, cruelty, and bes-
        tiality were so overpowering . . . I made the visit deliberately, in order to
        be in a position to give first-hand evidence of these things if ever, in the
        future, there develops a tendency to charge these allegations to propagan-
        da." Eisenhower, in a letter to Gen. George C. Marshall, April 15, 1945,
        after the liberation of the Ohrdruf concentration camp. The quotation
        is reproduced on the exterior of the United States Holocaust Memorial
        Museum in Washington, DC.

he uses smoke and mirrors: Eisenhower held the first televised press conference. "The Press at the White House, 1952-1963," White House Historical Association, https://www.whitehousehistory.org/the-press-at-the-white-house-1952-1963.

a new look: NSC 162/2: John Lewis Gaddis, *Strategies of Containment: A Critical Appraisal of American National Security Policy During the Cold War* (New York: Oxford University Press, 2005).

110   **"you have a row of dominos set up"**: Dwight D. Eisenhower, Press Conference, April 7, 1954.

in his farewell address: Dwight D. Eisenhower, "Farewell Address," January 17,1961, https://www.ourdocuments.gov/doc.php?flash=-false&doc=90&page=transcript.

he retires to the battlefield: Eisenhower National Historic Site, "Eisenhower at Gettysburg," National Park Service, https://www.nps.gov/eise/learn/historyculture/eisenhower-at-gettysburg.htm.

a simple soldier's casket: "Dwight D. Eisenhower's Final Post," Dwight D. Eisenhower Presidential Library, https://www.eisenhowerlibrary.gov/eisenhowers/dwight-d-eisenhowers-final-post.

111   **from at least frame 225**: *Report of the Warren Commission On the Assassination of President Kennedy,* 1st ed. (New York: McGraw-Hill, 1964).

my father tells me: Interview with Tom Rafferty, September, 2015.

112   **"words alone are not enough"**: John F. Kennedy, "Remarks Intended for Delivery to the Texas Democratic State Committee in the Municipal Auditorium in Austin, November 22, 1963 [Undelivered]," John F. Kennedy Presidential Library and Museum, https://www.jfklibrary.org/archives/other-resources/john-f-kennedy-speeches/austin-tx-undelivered-19631122.

numbers on a scale or a cartoon face: Eula Biss, "The Pain Scale," *Seneca Review,* Vol. 35, Issue 1, Spring 2005.

Kennedy spent his life in pain: Robert Dallek, "The Medical Ordeals of JFK's Life," *Atlantic,* December 2002.

the four-hour swim after PT-109 sank: Michael Granberry, "Man Saved from Drowning by John F. Kennedy Dies," *Los Angeles Times,* February 21, 1990.

he received last rites at least three times: Four, by some counts, and five, if post-assassination is included. Nik deCosta-Klipa, "JFK Had 5 Brushes with Death Before that Open-Air Dallas Car Ride," May 22, 2017, https://www.boston.com/news/history/2017/05/22/jfk-had-5-brushes-with-death-before-that-open-air-dallas-car-ride.

Surgeons operated on his back four times: T. Glenn Pait and Justin T. Dowdy, "John F. Kennedy's Back: Chronic Pain, Failed Surgeries, and the Story of Its Effects on His Life and Death," *Journal of Neurosurgery,* July 11, 2017, https://thejns.org/spine/view/journals/j-neurosurg-spine/27/3/article-p247.xml.

he never said a word about it: Lawrence K. Altman and Todd S. Purdum, "In J.F.K. File, Hidden Illness, Pain and Pills," *New York Times,* November 17, 2002.

He met Khrushchev in Vienna: Pait and Dowdy, "John F. Kennedy's Back."

113   **He was wearing his back brace in Dallas**: Ibid.

born from the Greek *algos*: "nostalgia, n." *OED Online,* (New York: Oxford University Press, March 2020), www.oed.com/view/Entry/128472.

114   **the average age of those boys**: Arthur G. Neal, *National Trauma and Collective Memory: Extraordinary Events in the American Experience* (Armonk, NY: M. E. Sharpe, 2005).

all the awards that matter: The Pulitzer Prize, twice (1975, 2003), the National Book Award (2002), the National Book Critic's Circle Award twice (1982, 1990), and a couple of dozen others. He's also an honorary Texas Ranger.

violating a ban on theatrical performances: Rob Hardy, "Cato," https://www.mountvernon.org/library/digitalhistory/digital-encyclopedia/article/cato/.

115   ***let us bear this awful corpse to Caesar***: Joseph Addison, *Cato*, Act V, Scene 1.

***boys, I need you,* Johnson calls**: Author visit to Lyndon B. Johnson National Historic Site, October, 2014.

Washington rides his horse in a snowstorm: White McKenzie Wallenborn, "George Washington's Terminal Illness: A Modern Medical Analysis of the Last Illness and Death of George Washington," Washington Papers, University of Virginia, https://washingtonpapers.org/resources/articles/illness/.

we may safely trust to temporary alliances: George Washington, "Farewell Address," September 17, 1796.

Norman Morrison: Oscar Patterson III, "The Living and the Dead: Robert McNamera and Five Lives of a Lost War," *Journal of American Culture,* Vol. 21, Issue 3, Fall 1998.

to drop his infant daughter: Ibid.

flames ten feet high: John-Paul Flintoff, "I Told Them to Be Brave," *Guardian,* October 15, 2010.

116   **Caro in an introduction discusses two threads**: Robert A. Caro, *The Years of Lyndon Johnson: The Path to Power.* (New York: Random House, 1982).

LBJ in 1928 in the South Texas town of Cotulla: Charles Peters, *Lyndon B. Johnson* (New York: Times Books, 2010).

dig through garbage piles to find grapefruit rinds: Ibid.

sending his cook Hercules back to Virginia: Blakemore, "George Washington Used Legal Loopholes to Avoid Freeing His Slaves."

117   **LBJ saying *we shall overcome*:** Lyndon B. Johnson, "Address to Congress," March 15, 1965.

118   **there are twelve men who know**: "Who Has Walked on the Moon?" *NASA Science,* June 3, 2019.

who had started his own club: Rick Perlstein, *Nixonland: The Rise of a President and the Fracturing of America* (New York: Scribner, 2008).

supposedly an accidental erasure: "Rose Mary Woods, Nixon's Secretary, Dies," *New York Times,* January 23, 2005.

119   **several thousand condolence letters**: Approximately 21,000 American military members were killed in the Vietnam conflict after Nixon's inauguration. National Archives, "Vietnam War U.S. Military Fatal Casualty Statistics,"https://www.archives.gov/research/military/vietnam-war/casualty-statistics.

his first inaugural address: Richard Nixon, "First Inaugural Address," January 20, 1969.

Haldeman's notes mentioned: Tom McNichol, "Richard Nixon's Last Secret," *Wired,* July, 2002.

120   **Alexander Haig said that "a sinister force"**: Lesley Oelsner, "Haig Says White House Feared 'Sinister Force' Ruined Tape But Now Feels Miss Woods Is to Blame," *New York Times,* December 7, 1973.

his father ran a gas station and grocery store: Michael Mello, "A Century Later, Nixon Legacy Carries On," *Orange County Register,* January 7, 2013.

more known for his cheering than his playing time: Alex Beggs, "Pumped-Up Politicians: The Most Athletic Presidents of All Time," *Vanity Fair,* September 12, 2012. Whittier College's mascot is Johnny Poet, and their teams are the Poets.

elected president of its bar association: Pamela B. Gann, "In Memoriam: Richard M. Nixon," *Duke Law Journal,* Vol. 44, No. 3, December 1994.

his five o'clock shadow dooming him: David Greenberg, "Torchlight Parades for the Television Age: The Presidential Debates as Political Ritual," *Daedalus,* Vol. 138, Issue 2, Spring, 2009.

121   **erased from the landscape in 2017**: Danny Lewis, "The Parking Garage Where Deep Throat Spilled the Beans on Watergate Is Being Torn Down," *Smithsonian Magazine*, January 10, 2017. As of the summer of 2020, the garage still stands.

122   **the Plumbers got up to their dirty tricks**: Dwight D. Murphey, "Nixon's White House Wars," *Journal of Social, Political, and Economic Studies*, Vol. 42, Issue 3/4, Fall 2017.

Daniel Ellsberg leaked the Pentagon Papers: Daniel Ellsberg, *Secrets: A Memoir of Vietnam and the Pentagon Papers* (New York: Viking, 2002).

123   ***Victory with honor***: Seth Offenbach, *The Conservative Movement and the Vietnam War: The Other Side of Vietnam* (London: Routledge, 2019).

You turned down the Lions and the Packers: Rob Crotty, "Green Bay Packer, Detroit Lion, or US President?" National Archives, February 2, 2011. https://prologue.blogs.archives.gov/2011/02/02/green-bay-packer-detroit-lion-or-us-president/.

you both stood there, frozen: Maurice Carroll, "Sound of Debate Off Air Nearly Half Hour: Ford and Carter Debate Economic Issue," *New York Times*, September 24, 1976.

124   **you know about a magic bullet**: "there is very persuasive evidence from the experts to indicate that the same bullet which pierced the president's throat also caused Governor Connally's wounds," *Report of the Warren Commission On the Assassination of President Kennedy*.

there is no Soviet domination: Bernard Gwertzman, "Ford Denies Moscow Dominates East Europe; Carter Rebuts Him," *New York Times*, October 7, 1976. At the time, the United States considered Poland, Bulgaria, Czechoslovakia, Hungary, and East Germany to be satellite states of the Soviet Union in Eastern Europe, part of the Iron Curtain of the Cold War.

126   ***All have sinned***: Epistle to the Romans, Chapter 2, Verse 23.

127   **when he takes the oath of office**: Jimmy Carter, "Inaugural Address," January 20, 1977.

he brings Egypt and Israel together: William B. Quandt, "Camp David and Peacemaking in the Middle East," *Political Science Quarterly*, Vol. 101, No. 3, 1986.

he returns Panama its own canal: Robert A. Strong, "Jimmy Carter and the Panama Canal Treaties," *Presidential Studies Quarterly*, Vol. 21, No. 2, April 1, 1991.

he sets what will become the United States Holocaust Memorial Museum into motion: Edward T. Linenthal, *Preserving Memory: The Struggle to Create America's Holocaust Museum* (New York: Columbia University Press, 2001).

he negotiates with his Soviet counterpart: Hedrick Smith, "U.S. and Soviet Sign Strategic Arms Treaty; Carter Urges Congress to Support Accord," *New York Times,* June 19, 1979.

he signs a blanket pardon: Allen Pusey, "Carter Pardons Vietnam-Era Draft Dodgers," *ABA Journal,* Vol. 100, Issue 1, January 2014.

128   **thirty-nine Santee Sioux**: One man had his death sentence commuted; the other thirty-eight were hung on December 26, 1862, in Mankato, Minnesota. "38," Layli Long Soldier, *Whereas* (Minneapolis: Graywolf Press, 2017).

130   **You startin' to tell my future?**: All dialogue attributed to Duke comes from films in which John Wayne died. In order of appearance: *Reap the Wild Wind,* directed by Cecil B. DeMille, Paramount, 1942; *The Fighting Seabees,* directed by Edward Ludwig, Republic Pictures, 1944; *Wake of the Red Witch,* directed by Edward Ludwig, Republic Pictures, 1948; *Sands of Iwo Jima,* directed by Allan Dwan, Republic Pictures, 1949; *The Alamo,* directed by John Wayne, Batjac Productions, 1960; *The Cowboys,* directed by Mark Rydell, Warner Brothers, 1972; and *The Shootist,* directed by Don Siegel, Paramount, 1976.

We are faced with the most evil enemy: All dialogue attributed to Reagan comes from speeches and statements by Ronald Reagan.

133   **Reagan's eyesight kept him home**: "Military Service of Ronald Reagan," Ronald Reagan Presidential Library and Museum, https://www.reaganlibrary.gov/sreference/military-service-of-ronald-reagan.

Wayne was deferred: Randy Roberts and James S. Olson, *John Wayne: American* (Lincoln, NE: Bison Books, 1997).

136   **when he was a pilot in the war**: Herbert S. Parmet, *George Bush: The Life of a Lone Star Yankee* (New York: Scribner, 1997).

he played in the first two College World Series: Herm Krabbenhoft, "The Complete Collegiate Baseball Record of George H. W. Bush," *Baseball Research Journal,* Vol. 46, Issue 2, Fall 2017.

Taft started this: Ibid.

Tinker to Evers to Bush: A play on "Tinker to Evers to Chance," a reference to Joe Tinker, Johnny Evers, and Frank Chance, the core of the Chicago Cubs defense at the beginning of the twentieth century. David Rapp, *Tinker to Evers to Chance: The Chicago Cubs and the Dawn of Modern America* (Chicago: University of Chicago Press, 2018).

He meets with their Prime Minister: "Sports People: Baseball; Bush to Jays' Opener," *New York Times,* March 28, 1990.

137   **it fell to him to meet with Babe Ruth**: Krabbenhoft, "The Complete Collegiate Baseball Record of George H. W. Bush."

to an adoring crowd, he spoke briefly: Babe Ruth, "Address to Fans on 'Babe Ruth Day' at Yankee Stadium," April 27, 1947. https://www.americanrhetoric.com/speeches/baberuthfarewelltobaseball.htm.

drills the Permian Basin himself: Parmet, *George Bush*.

his colleagues nickname him "Rubbers": Frank Rich, "Stag Party," *New York*, Vol. 45, Issue 10, April 2, 2012.

138   **in 1990, George wears a Texas Rangers jacket**: Brett Regan, "Nobody Threw Ceremonial First Pitch Strikes Quite Like President George H. W. Bush," *FanBuzz*, December 1, 2018. https://fanbuzz.com/mlb/president-george-h-w-bush-first-pitches/.

139   **the first president to have an e-mail address**: Patrick Novotny, *The Press in American Politics: 1787-2012* (Santa Barbara: Praeger, 2014).

his failure to intervene in Rwanda: Samantha Power, "Bystanders to Genocide," *The Atlantic*, Vol. 288, Issue 2, September, 2001.

there's a letter he wrote a long time ago: Bill Clinton, "The 1992 Campaign: A Letter By Clinton on His Draft Deferment: 'A War I Opposed and Despised.'" *New York Times*, February 13, 1992.

the first name inscribed: Derek Turner, "The First and Last Names on the Wall." *USO*, June 18, 2014, https://www.uso.org/stories/1715-the-first-and-the-last-names-on-the-wall.

140   **a deferment, 2-S**: Dan Balz, "Clinton and the Draft: Anatomy of a Controversy." *Washington Post*, September 13, 1992.

so he does what he can: Ibid.

the previous year's Tet Offensive: Mark Bowden, *Hue 1968: A Turning Point of the American War in Vietnam* (New York: Atlantic Monthly Press, 2017).

Nixon promises "an honorable end": Richard M. Nixon, "Presidential Nomination Acceptance Speech," August 8, 1968.

142   **he'll become the youngest governor in Arkansas history**: John Gartner, *In Search of Bill Clinton: A Psychological Biography* (New York: St. Martin's Press, 2008).

in twenty-eight years, he'll normalize diplomatic relations: Ann Devroy, "Clinton Opens Diplomatic Ties With Vietnam: Era of Official Enmity With Hanoi Closed in Step to Normalization," *Washington Post*, July 13, 1995.

143   **Ted Koppel dedicated an episode of *Nightline***: "A Conversation With Governor Bill Clinton," *Nightline,* ABC, February 12, 1992.

144   **interrupts the reading of *My Pet Goat:*** I have preserved the misreporting of the title, which is actually "The Pet Goat." Ron Charles, "Another

Tale from Sept. 11: 'Pet Goat.'" *Washington Post*, September 10, 2011.

a bullhorn, future artifact: Kenneth T. Walsh, "George W. Bush's 'Bullhorn' Moment," *US News and World Report*, April 25, 2013.

I can hear you, **he says**: Ibid.

wanted, dead or alive: Toby Harnden, "Bin Laden Is Wanted: Dead or Alive, Bush Says," *Telegraph*, September 18, 2001.

I remember reading a first responder: I hope that you and my editors will forgive this, but I cannot find confirmation of this, although I have a distinct memory of reading this in the fall of 2001. I have the sense that it was in either *Slate* or *Salon*, but searches of their archives turn up nothing.

his father, twelve years earlier: George H. W. Bush, "Address to America," January 16, 1991.

145   **sometimes you have to suspend habeas corpus**: Robert O. Faith, "Public Necessity or Military Convenience? Reevaluating Lincoln's Suspensions of the Writ of Habeas Corpus During the Civil War," *Civil War History*, Vol. 62, No. 3, 2016.

    the joker's face as Kanye states: Josh Terry, "10 Years Ago Today, Kanye West Said 'George Bush Doesn't Care About Black People,'" *Redeye*, September 2, 2015, https://www.chicagotribune.com/redeye/redeye-kanye-west-katrina-telethon-george-bush-black-people-20150902-htmlstory.html.

    as he flies away, the crowd will sing: Tabassum Zakaria, "Bush Exits White House, Goes Home to Texas," *Reuters*, January 20, 2009.

147   **the static live shot of the podium**: Macon Phillips, "Osama Bin Laden Dead," May 2, 2011, https://obamawhitehouse.archives.gov/blog/2011/05/02/osama-bin-laden-dead.

    every Democrat since Truman: L. Manchikanti et. al, "Evolution of US Health Care Reform," *Pain Physician*, Vol. 20, No. 3, March, 2017.

    he paused while speaking in Charleston: By my inexpert timing, he pauses for twelve seconds, an eternity in public speaking. C-SPAN, "President Obama sings Amazing Grace (C-SPAN)," *YouTube*. June 26, 2015. https://www.youtube.com/watch?v=IN05jVNBs64.

    them chanting *Jews will not replace us:* Susan Svrluga, "Spender Leads Torchlight Rally at U-Va," *Washington Post*, October 8, 2017.

148   **him I heard in a small town in Virginia**: Chelyen Davis, "26,000 Hear Obama at University of Mary Washington," *Free-Lance Star*, September 28, 2008.

149   **Trump gives everything the same name**: Erin Durkin, "Here's How Much Donald Trump Loves Naming Things After Himself," *New York Daily News*, July 27, 2016.

150   **"I alone can fix it"**: Donald J. Trump, "Presidential Nomination Acceptance Speech," July 21, 2016.

      He gives lots of names: "List of Nicknames Used by Donald Trump," *Wikipedia*, Wikimedia Foundation, May 15, 2020, https://en.wikipedia.org/w/index.php?title=List_of_nicknames_used_by_Donald_Trump.

      one senator stated: Aaron Blake, "Lamar Alexander's Yes-He-Did-It Statement on Trump, Annotated," *Washington Post*, January 31, 2020.

151   **the number of baby boys named Donald**: Confirmed via the Social Security Name Index, https://www.ssa.gov/cgi-bin/babyname.cgi.

153   **the Virginia Reel that George and Martha danced**: Phil Jamison, *Hoedowns, Reels, and Frolics: Roots and Branches of Southern Appalachian Dance* (Champaign, IL: University of Illinois Press, 2015).

      President Ford declared that the bells of America should ring: Gerald Ford, "Proclamation 4446—Bicentennial Independence Day," June 29, 1976, https://www.presidency.ucsb.edu/documents/proclamation-4446-bicentennial-independence-day.

      in an address he made in Philadelphia: Gerald Ford, "Remarks of Gerald R. Ford in Philadelphia, Pennsylvania (Bicentennial Celebration)," July 4, 1976, https://www.fordlibrarymuseum.gov/library/speeches/760645.asp.

154   **the planning is underway**: Both chambers of Congress unanimously passed the United States Semiquincentennial Commission Act in 2016. The commission is composed of members of Congress, private citizens, and leaders of federal agencies. https://www.america250.org/.

      Graham . . . had developed a style of dance: Anna Kisselgoff, "Martha Graham Dies at 96: A Revolutionary in Dance," *New York Times*, April 2, 1991.

      a girl from Michigan named Betty Bloomer: Anna Kisselgoff, "Martha Graham Recalls Years With Former Pupil, Betty Ford," *New York Times*, August 10, 1974.

      Decades earlier, Graham had said: *A Dancer's World*, directed by Peter Glushanok, WQED, 1957.

      she cited an old saying: "Dancer Martha Graham Awarded Presidential Medal of Freedom by President Ford," *NBC News*, NBCUniversal Media. 2 Jan. 1974.

      I could communicate using gestures: National Institute on Deafness and Other Communication Disorders, "Speech and Language Developmental Milestones," National Institutes of Health. https://www.nidcd.nih.gov/health/speech-and-language.

155   **"you got a price to pay"**: *Reporting Vietnam*, Newseum, 2015-2016.

156 **once, in a library in the nation's capital**: Author visit to the Society of the Cincinnati headquarters, October 9, 2014.

a letter written by Washington declining an honorary position: George Washington, "Circular Letter," October 31, 1786, reprinted in *Register of the Society of the Cincinnati of Maryland Brought Down to February 22, 1897* (Baltimore: A. Horn and Co., 1897).

Appendix: Reading List

Joseph J. Ellis, *His Excellency: George Washington* (New York: Alfred A. Knopf, 2004).

David McCullough, *John Adams* (New York: Simon and Schuster, 2001).

R. B. Bernstein, *Thomas Jefferson* (New York: Oxford University Press, 2003)

Garry Wills, *James Madison* (New York: Times Books; Henry Holt and Co., 2002)

Gary Hart, *James Monroe* (New York: Times Books; Henry Holt and Co., 2005)

Paul C. Nagel, *John Quincy Adams: A Public Life, a Private Life* (New York: Alfred A. Knopf, 1997).

Jon Meacham, *American Lion: Andrew Jackson in the White House* (New York: Random House, 2008).

Joel H. Silbey, *Martin Van Buren and the Emergence of American Popular Politics* (Princeton: Princeton University Press, 1984).

Robert M. Owens, *Mr. Jefferson's Hammer: William Henry Harrison and the Origins of American Indian Policy* (Norman: University of Oklahoma Press, 2007).

Edward P. Crapol, *John Tyler: The Accidental President* (Chapel Hill: University of North Carolina Press, 2006).

Walter R. Borneman, *Polk: The Man Who Transformed the Presidency and America* (New York: Random House, 2009).

Jack K. Bauer, *Zachary Taylor: Soldier, Planter, Statesman of the Old Southwest* (Baton Rouge: LSU Press, 1993).

Robert J. Rayback, *Millard Fillmore: Biography of a President* (Newtown, CT: American Political Biography Press, 1959).

Roy Franklin Nichols, *Franklin Pierce: Young Hickory of the Granite Hills* (Philadelphia: University of Pennsylvania Press, 1939).

Philip Shriver Klein, *President James Buchanan: A Biography* (State College, PA: Penn State University Press, 1990).

Ronald C. White Jr., *A. Lincoln* (New York: Random House, 2009).

Hans L. Trefousse, *Andrew Johnson* (New York: W. W. Norton & Company, 1997).

Jean Edward Smith, *Grant* (New York: Simon and Schuster, 2002).

Ari Hoogenboom, *Rutherford B. Hayes: Warrior and President* (Lawrence, KS: University Press of Kansas, 1995).

Allan Peskin, *Garfield* (Kent, OH: Kent State University Press, 1978).

Thomas C. Reeves, *Gentleman Boss: The Life of Chester Alan Arthur* (Newtown, CT: American Political Biography Press, 1991).

H. Paul Jeffers, *An Honest President: The Life and Presidencies of Grover Cleveland* (New York: William Morrow, 2000).

Charles W. Calhoun, *Benjamin Harrison* (New York: Times Books, 2005).

H. Wayne Morgan, *William McKinley and His America* (Kent, OH: Kent State University Press, 1998).

Kathleen Dalton, *Theodore Roosevelt: A Strenuous Life* (New York: Knopf, 2002).

Judith Icke Anderson, *William Howard Taft: An Intimate History* (New York: W. W Norton & Company, 1981).

John Milton Cooper Jr., *Woodrow Wilson* (New York: Knopf, 2009).

Andrew Sinclair, *The Available Man: The Life Behind the Masks of Warren Gamaliel Harding* (New York: Macmillan, 1967).

Robert Sobel, *Coolidge: An American Enigma* (Washington, D.C.: Regnery Publishing, 2000).

David Burner, *Herbert Hoover: A Public Life* (New York: Knopf, 1979).

H. W. Brands, *Traitor to His Class: The Privileged Life and Radical Presidency of Franklin Delano Roosevelt* (New York: Doubleday, 2008).

David McCullough, *Truman* (New York: Simon and Schuster, 1992).

Geoffrey Perret, *Eisenhower* (New York: Random House, 1999).

Robert Dallek, *An Unfinished Life: John F. Kennedy, 1917-1963* (Boston: Little, Brown and Company, 2003).

Irwin Unger, *LBJ: A Life* (Hoboken, NJ: Wiley, 1999).

Conrad Black, *Richard M. Nixon: A Life in Full* (New York: Public Affairs, 2007).

Douglas G. Brinkley, *Gerald Ford* (New York: Times Books, 2007).

Peter G. Bourne, *Jimmy Carter: A Comprehensive Biography from Plains to Post-Presidency* (New York: Scribner, 1997).

John Patrick Diggins, *Ronald Reagan: Fate, Freedom, and the Making of History* (New York: W. W. Norton & Company, 2008).

Herbert S. Parmet, *George Bush: The Life of a Lone Star Yankee* (New York: Scribner, 1997).

John Gartner, *In Search of Bill Clinton: A Psychological Biography* (New York: Macmillan, 2009).

Jacob Weisberg, *The Bush Tragedy* (New York: Random House, 2008).

David Maraniss, *Barack Obama: The Story* (New York: Simon and Schuster, 2012).

Michael Kranish, *Trump Revealed: An American Journey of Ambition, Ego, Money, and Power* (New York: Scribner, 2016).

Acknowledgments

I am deeply indebted to Christine E. Kelly and Danilo John Thomas at Baobab Press, who worked patiently and thoughtfully with this manuscript. In a chaotic time for a protean subject, they lit the way forward.

Thanks to the editors who published essays from this book in literary magazines: Jessica Berger and James Tadd Adcox (*Always Crashing*), Carissa Halston (*apt*), Katy Turner (*Bennington Review*), Dinty W. Moore (*Brevity*), Andrew Keating (*Cobalt*), Susannah Clark (*The Collapsar*), Judith Gapp (*Dark Wood*), Lisa Nikolidakis (*The Evansville Review*), Naomi Washer (*Ghost Proposal*), Cumi Ikeda and Gavin Jenkins (*Hot Metal Bridge*), Leslie Jill Patterson (*Iron Horse Literary Review*), Ryan Ridge (*Juked*), Ann Beman (*Los Angeles Review*), Gordon Krupsky (*The MacGuffin*), Kate Lorenz (*Parcel*), Lucas Church (*Pinball*), Amy Monticello (*Prime Number Magazine*), Baker Lawley (*The Razor*), John-Michael Rivera (*Shadowbox*), Sarah Einstein (*Signal Mountain Review*), and Terry L. Kennedy (*storySouth*). Special thanks to Erin Stalcup at *Waxwing*, who sent a well-timed e-mail in December of 2016 that saved this project.

Thanks to Warren Rochelle, Laura Bylenok, Jon Pineda, Rachel Levy, and everyone in the Department of English, Linguistics, and Communication of the University of Mary Washington. Gwen Hale let me write the first full draft of this book in an empty office in UMW's Writing Center during my sabbatical. My students give me the chance to think about nonfiction writing every single day.

I had the good fortune to have a congress of librarians on my side while writing this, including Jack Bales, Rosemary Arneson, and Peter Catlin at Simpson Library, UMW; Adam Zimmerli, Tara Franzetti, and everyone at the East End Branch of the Richmond Public Library; Ralph Oppenheim at the Middlesex County Public Library; Matthew Schuler at Iowa State University, who unearthed and scanned the WPA report on Carroll County for me; and Ellen Clark and Rachel Jirka at the Society of the Cincinnati in Washington, DC, who showed me an amazing assortment of George Washington manuscripts and artifacts.

My own Federal Writers Project would include B.J. Hollars, Joni Tevis, Brian Oliu, Christopher Cokinos, Chelsea Biondolillo, Hugh Sheehy (who heard about the reading project and said he hoped I got a book out of it), Erin Lyndal Martin, MC Hyland, Jennifer Pemberton, Joey Franklin, Elena Passarello, Patrick Madden, Deb Marquart, Berry Grass, Felicia Zamora, Michael Martone, Tessa Fontaine, Andrew Beck Grace, Jeff Bean, Sonja Livingston, Scott Russell Sanders, and Jason McCall.

Andrew Jackson had his Kitchen Cabinet; I have Josh Baze, Zach Baze, Phil Kellum, Trey Hock, and Bill Kraai.

You could probably convince most partners to go to places like Mount Vernon and Monticello. Elizabeth Wade not only went there, but also went to the Martin Van Buren National Historic Site, Chester A. Arthur's grave, and Rutherford B. Hayes's house (twice!). For that and a hundred other reasons, I am grateful beyond measure.

Photo Credit: Elizabeth Wade

Born in Kansas City, Missouri, Colin Rafferty grew up on the Kansas side (which makes a difference). In third grade, he unhesitatingly told an autograph dealer that the label on a Lincoln autograph was wrong—he was the sixteenth president, not the seventeenth. Later, Rafferty attended land grant universities (Kansas State, Iowa State) and eventually got an MFA from the University of Alabama. He writes about monuments and memorials, presidents, and more generally, public and private histories. In doing research for *Execute the Office*, he visited the graves of twenty-eight presidents, toured the homes of another sixteen, and, for reasons still unbeknownst to him, was allowed to handle a four-page letter written by George Washington. Rafferty has taught nonfiction writing at the University of Mary Washington since 2008, developing classes on nonfiction of place, the lyric essay, and writing for multimedia. Since 2012, he has lived in Richmond, Virginia, with his wife, Elizabeth, and their dog in the same neighborhood where Patrick Henry gave the "give me liberty or give me death" speech in the presence of two future presidents. He is surrounded by history.